Uncover 2

Combo B

Ben Goldstein • Ceri Jones
with Kathryn O'Dell

Student's Book

CB082893

CAMBRIDGE UNIVERSITY PRESS
Discovery EDUCATION

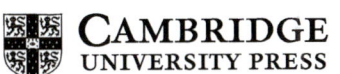

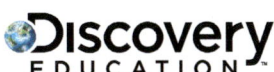

CAMBRIDGE
UNIVERSITY PRESS

University Printing House, Cambridge CB2 8BS, United Kingdom

One Liberty Plaza, 20th Floor, New York, NY 10006, USA

477 Williamstown Road, Port Melbourne, VIC 3207, Australia

314–321, 3rd Floor, Plot 3, Splendor Forum, Jasola District Centre, New Delhi – 110025, India

103 Penang Road, #05-06/07, Visioncrest Commercial, Singapore 238467

Cambridge University Press is part of the University of Cambridge.

It furthers the University's mission by disseminating knowledge in the pursuit of education, learning and research at the highest international levels of excellence.

www.cambridge.org
Information on this title: www.cambridge.org/9781107515062

© Cambridge University Press 2015

This publication is in copyright. Subject to statutory exception and to the provisions of relevant collective licensing agreements, no reproduction of any part may take place without the written permission of Cambridge University Press.

First published 2015

20 19 18 17 16 15 14 13

Printed in Great Britain by CPI Group (UK) Ltd, Croydon CR0 4YY

A catalog record for this publication is available from the British Library.

ISBN 978-1-107-49320-9 Student's Book 2
ISBN 978-1-107-49323-0 Student's Book with Online Workbook and Online Practice 2
ISBN 978-1-107-51505-5 Combo 2A
ISBN 978-1-107-51506-2 Combo 2B
ISBN 978-1-107-49331-5 Teacher's Book 2
ISBN 978-1-107-49328-5 Workbook with Online Practice 2
ISBN 978-1-107-49338-4 Presentation Plus Disc 2
ISBN 978-1-107-49333-9 Class Audio CDs 2
ISBN 978-1-107-49335-3 DVD 2

Additional resources for this publication at www.cambridge.org/uncover

The publishers have no responsibility for the persistence or accuracy of URLs for external or third-party Internet websites referred to in this publication, and do not guarantee that any content on such websites is, or will remain, accurate or appropriate. Information regarding prices, travel timetables, and other factual information given in this work is correct at the time of first printing but the publishers do not guarantee the accuracy of such information thereafter.

Art direction, book design, layout services, and photo research: QBS Learning
Audio production: John Marshall Media

Acknowledgments

Many teachers, coordinators, and educators shared their opinions, their ideas, and their experience to help create *Uncover*. The authors and publisher would like to thank the following people and their schools for their help in shaping the series.

In Mexico:
María Nieves Maldonado Ortiz (Colegio Enrique Rébsamen); Héctor Guzmán Pineda (Liceo Europeo); Alfredo Salas López (Campus Universitario Siglo XXI); Rosalba Millán Martínez (IIPAC [Instituto Torres Quintero A.C.]); Alejandra Rubí Reyes Badillo (ISAS [Instituto San Angel del Sur]); José Enrique Gutiérrez Escalante (Centro Escolar Zama); Gabriela Juárez Hernández (Instituto de Estudios Básicos Amado Nervo); Patricia Morelos Alonso (Instituto Cultural Ingles, S.C.); Martha Patricia Arzate Fernández, (Colegio Valladolid); Teresa González, Eva Marina Sánchez Vega (Colegio Salesiano); María Dolores León Ramírez de Arellano, (Liceo Emperadores Aztecas); Esperanza Medina Cruz (Centro Educativo Francisco Larroyo); Nubia Nelly Martínez García (Salesiano Domingo Savio); Diana Gabriela González Benítez (Colegio Ghandi); Juan Carlos Luna Olmedo (Centro Escolar Zama); Dulce María Pascual Granados (Esc. Juan Palomo Martínez); Roberto González, Fernanda Audirac (Real Life English Center); Rocio Licea (Escuela Fundación Mier y Pesado); Diana Pombo (Great Union Institute); Jacobo Cortés Vázquez (Instituto María P. de Alvarado); Michael John Pryor (Colegio Salesiano Anáhuac Chapalita)

In Brazil:
Renata Condi de Souza (Colégio Rio Branco); Sônia Maria Bernal Leites (Colégio Rio Branco); Élcio Souza (Centro Universitário Anhaguera de São Paulo); Patricia Helena Nero (Private teacher); Célia Elisa Alves de Magalhães (Colégio Cruzeiro-Jacarepaguá); Lilia Beatriz Freitas Gussem (Escola Parque-Gávea); Sandra Maki Kuchiki (Easy Way Idiomas); Lucia Maria Abrão Pereira Lima (Colégio Santa Cruz-São Paulo); Deborah de Castro Ferroz de Lima Pinto (Mundinho Segmento); Clara Vianna Prado (Private teacher); Ligia Maria Fernandes Diniz (Escola Internacional de Alphaville); Penha Aparecida Gaspar Rodrigues (Colégio Salesiano Santa Teresinha); Silvia Castelan (Colégio Santa Catarina de Sena); Marcelo D'Elia (The Kids Club Guarulhos); Malyina Kazue Ono Leal (Colégio Bandeirantes); Nelma de Mattos Santana Alves (Private teacher); Mariana Martins Machado (Britannia Cultural); Lilian Bluvol Vaisman (Curso Oxford); Marcelle Belfort Duarte (Cultura Inglesa-Duque de Caxias); Paulo Dantas (Britannia International English); Anauã Carmo Vilhena (York Language Institute); Michele Amorim Estellita (Lemec – Lassance Modern English Course); Aida Setton (Colégio Uirapuru); Maria Lucia Zaorob (CEL-LEP); Marisa Veiga Lobato (Interlíngua Idiomas); Maria Virgínia Lebrón (Independent consultant); Maria Luiza Carmo (Colégio Guilherme Dumont Villares/CEL-LEP); Lucia Lima (Independent consultant); Malyina Kazue Ono Leal (Colégio Bandeirantes); Debora Schisler (Seven Idiomas); Helena Nagano (Cultura Inglesa); Alessandra de Campos (Alumni); Maria Lúcia Sciamarelli (Colégio Divina Providência); Catarina Kruppa (Cultura Inglesa); Roberto Costa (Freelance teacher/consultant); Patricia McKay Aronis (CEL-LEP); Claudia Beatriz Cavalieri (By the World Idiomas); Sérgio Lima (Vermont English School); Rita Miranda (IBI – [Instituto Batista de Idiomas]); Maria de Fátima Galery (Britain English School); Marlene Almeida (Teacher Trainer Consultant); Flávia Samarane (Colégio Logosófico); Maria Tereza Vianna (Greenwich Schools); Daniele Brauer (Cultura Inglesa/AMS Idiomas); Allessandra Cierno (Colégio Santa Dorotira); Helga Silva Nelken (Greenwich Schools/Colégio Edna Roriz); Regina Marta Bazzoni (Britain English School); Adriano Reis (Greenwich Schools); Vanessa Silva Freire de Andrade (Private teacher); Nilvane Guimarães (Colégio Santo Agostinho)

In Ecuador:
Santiago Proaño (Independent teacher trainer); Tania Abad (UDLA [Universidad de Las Americas]); Rosario Llerena (Colegio Isaac Newton); Paúl Viteri (Colegio Andino); Diego Maldonado (Central University); Verónica Vera (Colegio Tomás Moro); Mónica Sarauz (Colegio San Gabriel); Carolina Flores (Colegio APCH); Boris Cadena, Vinicio Reyes (Colegio Benalcázar); Deigo Ponce (Colegio Gonzaga); Byron Freire (Colegio Nuestra Señora del Rosario)

The authors and publisher would also like to thank the following contributors, script writers, and collaborators for their inspired work in creating *Uncover*:
Anna Whitcher, Janet Gokay, Kathryn O'Dell, Lynne Robertson, and Dana Henricks

Unit	Vocabulary	Grammar	Listening	Conversation (Useful language)
6 Home, Sweet Home pp. 54–63	■ Furniture and other household items ■ Household appliances	■ Comparative and superlative adjectives and adverbs ■ *should (not), (not) have to, must (not)* Grammar reference p. 111	■ A clothing emergency	■ Asking for and offering help
7 Visions of the Future pp. 64–73	■ Computers and communication ■ Technology verbs	■ *will* and *won't* for predictions ■ Adverbs of possibility ■ First conditional with *will (not)*, *may (not)*, and *might (not)* Grammar reference p. 112	■ They're always coming out with something new.	■ Asking for and giving instructions
8 The Choices We Make pp. 74–83	■ Life events ■ Containers and materials	■ *be going to* and *will* ■ Present continuous and simple present for future Grammar reference p. 113	■ An eco-project	■ Agreeing and disagreeing
9 Watch Out! pp. 84–93	■ Accident and injury verbs ■ Parts of the body	■ Present perfect statements with regular and irregular verbs ■ Present perfect questions ■ Present perfect vs. simple past Grammar reference p. 114	■ I'm accident-prone.	■ Reacting to good and bad news
10 Have Fun! pp. 94–103	■ Free-time activities ■ Adjectives of feeling	■ Indefinite pronouns ■ *too* and *enough* Grammar reference p. 115	■ I'll never forget . . .	■ Making and responding to suggestions

Units 6–10 Review Game pp. 104–105

Writing	Reading	Video	Accuracy and fluency	Speaking outcomes
An email about your house	*A Home in the Jungle* Reading to write: *My House* Culture: *Life on the Water*	*A Cool Life* *Which do you prefer – houses or apartments?* *Moving House*	Using *must* for obligation Pronouncing the letters *er* and *or*	I can . . . identify rooms in a house and household items compare two or more rooms identify and talk about household appliances ask for and offer help talk about the kind of house I'd like to live in
An opinion paragraph	*Computers: A Big Past, A Small Future* Reading to write: *How do you think people will listen to music in the future?* Culture: *Television Grows Up . . . and Down!*	*A Pizza Robot* *How important is your cell phone?* *Music Sharing* *The Secret of the Pyramids* (CLIL Project p. 119)	First conditional vs. simple present Different sounds for the letters *ou* Using commas with *if* clauses	talk about computers and technology make predictions about the future talk about how to use technology ask for and give instructions talk about how I watch TV today and in the future
An application letter	*Life in the Outback* Reading to write: *Farah's Application Letter* Culture: *A Summer in Alaska*	*A School at Home* *What are you going to do when you leave school?* *Time for an Adventure!*	Present continuous for future arrangements The vowel sound of *will* and *we'll* Using *think*, *probably*, and *maybe* with *will*	I can . . . identify and talk about life events discuss future plans and predictions talk about future plans and scheduled events agree and disagree with someone talk about places I'd like to volunteer
An email to refuse an invitation	*It's Hard Being a Teen!* Reading to write: *Your Invitation* Culture: *Beware of the Amazon!*	*Danger in Our Food* *Have you ever had an accident?* *A Deadly Job*	The present perfect with *never* Forming past participles The sound of *have* in Wh- questions Using accident and injury words as both nouns and verbs	I can . . . talk about accidents and injuries talk about things I have and haven't done ask, answer, and give details about things I've done react to good and bad news talk about dangerous animals
An invitation	*Jodi's Blog* Reading to write: *Your Invitation* Culture: *April Fool's!*	*A New York City Food Tour* *How do you celebrate your birthday?* *Punkin Chunkin!* *An Ancient Answer* (CLIL Project p. 120)	Indefinite pronouns with *any-* in negative sentences The sound of the letters *gh*	I can . . . talk about free-time activities talk about weekend plans describe feelings and situations with *too* and *enough* make and respond to suggestions talk about April Fool's Day and jokes

6 Home, Sweet HOME

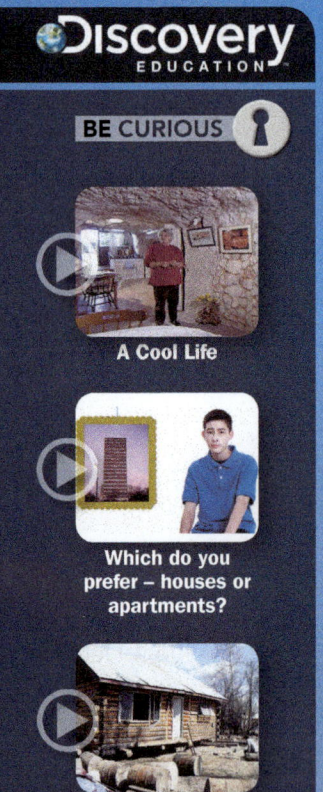

Discovery EDUCATION

BE CURIOUS

- A Cool Life
- Which do you prefer – houses or apartments?
- Moving House

1. What is this house like?
2. Who do you think lives here?
3. Would you want to live in a house like this? Why or why not?

UNIT CONTENTS

Vocabulary Furniture and other household items; household appliances
Grammar Comparative and superlative adjectives and adverbs; *should* (*not*), (*not*) *have to*, *must* (*not*)
Listening A clothing emergency

Vocabulary: Furniture and other household items

1. Match the words with the correct pictures.

a. a bed   c. a chair   e. a dresser   g. a shower   i. a table   ✓k. an armchair
b. a bookcase   d. a desk   f. a mirror   h. a sofa   j. a toilet   l. cabinets

LIVING ROOM   KITCHEN   BEDROOM   BATHROOM

1. k   2. ☐   3. ☐   4. ☐   5. ☐   6. ☐   7. ☐   8. ☐   9. ☐   10. ☐   11. ☐   12. ☐

2. Listen, check, and repeat.

3. Answer the questions with the words in Exercise 1.

1. Which items do you sit on?
   _____
2. Which items do you put things in?
   _____
3. Which items do you put things on?
   _____
4. Which items do you get into?
   _____
5. Which item do you look into?
   _____

> **Say it RIGHT!**
> The letters **er** and **or** can make the /ər/ sound. Listen to the sentence.
>
> *A photo of an act**or** is ov**er** my bed.*
>
> Listen to the words in Exercise 1 again. Which words have the /ər/ sound? What letters make the sound?

4. Work with a partner. Describe the furniture and items in Exercise 1.

> The armchair is big. It's brown and blue.

Speaking: Your house

5. YOUR TURN Which things from Exercise 1 are in your house? What other things do you have? Make a list.

> *Kitchen: cabinets, two chairs, . . .*

6. Work with a partner. Tell your partner about the things in your house.

> There isn't a table in our kitchen. There are a lot of cabinets. We have two chairs by the window . . .

Workbook, p. 36

Reading A Home in the Jungle; My House; Life on the Water
Conversation Asking for and offering help
Writing An email about your house

UNUSUAL Rooms

A Home in the JUNGLE

In the middle of the Amazon rain forest, with **monkeys**, **snakes**, and **tropical birds**, there's a very unusual place. Twenty meters up in the trees is the Ariaú Amazon Towers Hotel – the biggest treetop hotel in the world.

Walking paths connect two restaurants, two theaters, two swimming pools, and many guest rooms. You climb high on the paths to get to the standard rooms. Each room has a bedroom and a bathroom. Climb farther to get to the tree houses and Tarzan suites. Each of these has a bedroom, a bathroom, a living room, and a balcony with amazing views of the Amazon.

The Amazon River isn't far away, and visitors can see the "Meeting of the Waters." Two of the most powerful rivers in the Amazon, the Rio Negro and Rio Solimões, meet here. The black water of the Rio Negro is darker than the brown water of the Rio Solimões, and you can see both rivers side by side. The waters of the two rivers don't mix because the Rio Solimões runs more slowly than the Rio Negro.

It's a long way up, but a stay at the hotel is worth the climb!

Reading: An article about an unusual hotel

1. Look at the photos. What do you see? Where do you think it is?

2. Read and listen to the article. Why is the hotel unusual?

3. Read the article again. Answer the questions.
   1. Which animals live near the hotel?
      _____
   2. How high up in the trees is the hotel?
      _____
   3. What rooms do tree houses and Tarzan suites have?
      _____
   4. What is the "Meeting of the Waters"?
      _____

4. **YOUR TURN** Work with a partner. Would you like to stay in a treetop hotel? Why or why not?

   > I'd like to stay in a treetop hotel! I love nature and animals.

   > I wouldn't like it because . . .

DID YOU KNOW...?
The Rio Negro is home to the amazing pink dolphin, one of the rarest animals in the world.

Grammar: Comparative and superlative adjectives and adverbs

5. Complete the chart.

Use comparative adjectives and adverbs to show how two things are different from each other.
Use superlative adjectives and adverbs to compare three or more things.

	Comparative		Superlative	
Adjectives	dark → dark**er** powerful → **more** good → **better**	big → _____ bad → **worse**	dark → _____ popular → _____ good → **the best**	big → **the big**gest bad → **the worst**
	The Rio Negro is _____ than the Rio Solimões.		The bathroom is **the darkest** room in the hotel.	
Adverbs	fast → _____ far → far**ther** well → **better**	slowly → _____ badly → **worse**	fast → **the fastest** far → _____ well → _____	slowly → **the most slowly** badly → **the worst**
	The Rio Solimões runs **more slowly than** the Rio Negro.		The water runs _____ in the summer.	

> Check your answers: Grammar reference, p. 111

6. Complete the sentences with the comparative adjectives or adverbs.

1. Brazil is ___*bigger than*___ (big) Mexico.
2. The Rio Negro runs _____ (fast) the Rio Solimões.
3. A vacation in the Amazon is _____ (exciting) a vacation in Antarctica.
4. The furniture in my room is _____ (good) the furniture in your room.
5. We got _____ (wet) our parents on the hike because they used umbrellas.

7. Circle the correct words.

In Spain, I toured the Guadix cave homes with my sister. They are some of the ¹**strangest** / **more strangely** homes in the world. People live in cave houses there. The houses are ²**more dark** / **darker** than normal houses because they don't have many windows.

In the summer, the caves are ³**cooler** / **coolest** than normal homes, and in winter they are ⁴**the warmer** / **warmer**.

Our tour guide spoke ⁵**quickest** / **more quickly** than most tour guides. He talked the ⁶**faster** / **fastest** near the end of the tour. My sister understood the guide ⁷**better** / **best** than I did, so she repeated everything ⁸**slower** / **more slowly** for me.

Speaking: Compare!

8. YOUR TURN Discuss the questions with a partner.

1. Who studies longer at night?
2. Who is better at sports?

> I study for an hour at night.

> I study for two hours. I study longer than you.

9. Join another pair. Compare your answers to Exercise 8. Then answer these questions.

1. Who studies the longest at night?
2. Who is the best at sports?

> Jack studies for four hours at night. He studies the longest.

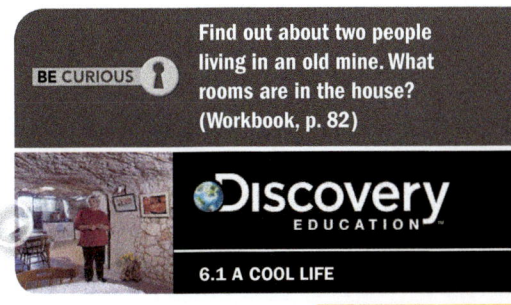

BE CURIOUS Find out about two people living in an old mine. What rooms are in the house? (Workbook, p. 82)

Discovery EDUCATION

6.1 A COOL LIFE

Things That PLUG IN

Listening: A clothing emergency

1. Who washes your clothes? Do you wash your own clothes?

2. Listen to Jackie tell her sister Chloe about her clothes. What's wrong with her pants? With her sweater?

3. Listen again and circle the correct answers.
   1. Jackie washed her dark and light clothes _____.
      a. together   b. separately   c. by hand
   2. Jackie's sweater is made of _____.
      a. cotton   b. jean material   c. wool
   3. Jackie washed her clothes on _____.
      a. hot   b. warm   c. cold
   4. Jackie learned how to fix her sweater from _____.
      a. her sister   b. a website   c. a label

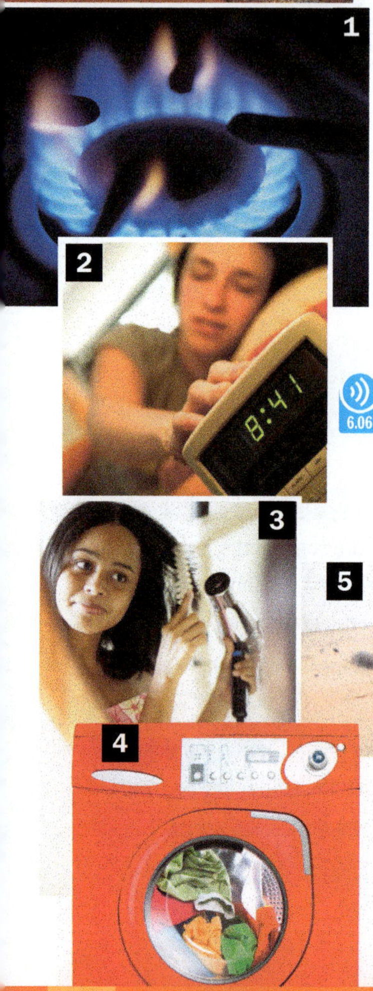

Vocabulary: Household appliances

4. Write the words next to the correct numbers. Then listen and check your answers.

a dishwasher	a microwave	a toaster	an alarm clock
a hair dryer	a refrigerator	a vacuum cleaner	an iron
a lamp	✓ a stove	a washing machine	an oven

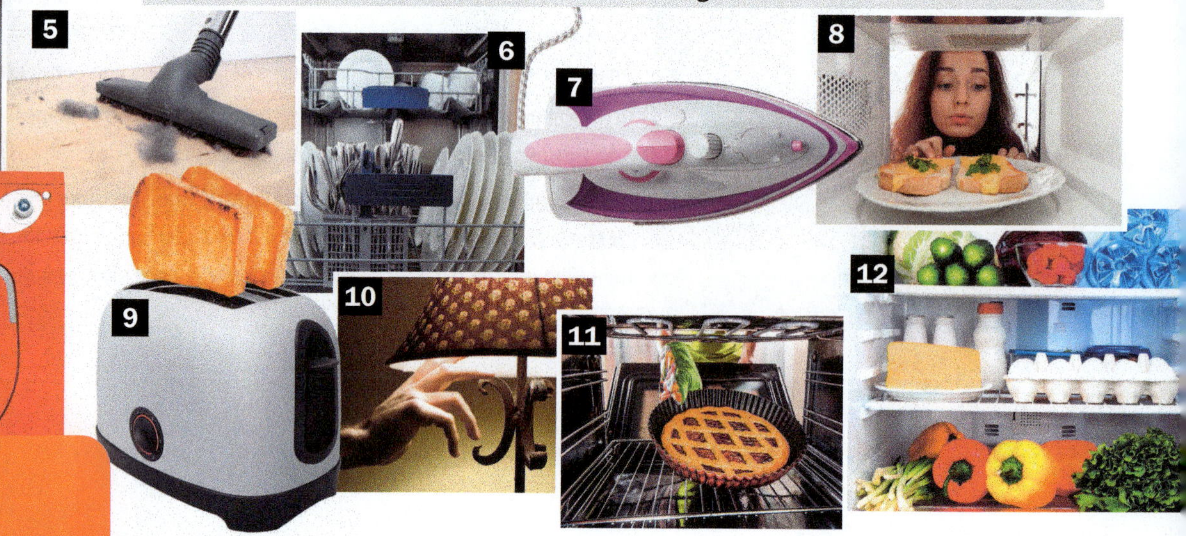

1. ___a stove___   5. _____   9. _____
2. _____   6. _____   10. _____
3. _____   7. _____   11. _____
4. _____   8. _____   12. _____

NOTICE IT
Fridge is short for *refrigerator*.

5. **YOUR TURN** Work with a partner. In what rooms do you use each of the household appliances in Exercise 4? How often do you use them?

> I use the stove in the kitchen. I use it two times a week.

58 | Unit 6

Grammar: should (not), (not) have to, must (not)

6. Complete the chart.

Use should not for advice and recommendations. Use have to for responsibilities.
Use not have to for things that are not required. Use must for obligation. Use must not for prohibition.

Affirmative	Negative
You _____ **wash** dark clothes separately. **She should look** at the labels.	You **shouldn't wash** darker clothes with lighter ones. She _____ **put** it in a sunny room.
You _____ **choose** the temperature first. It **has to be** cool.	You **don't have to wash** it by hand. It _____ **be** cold.
You **must use** cold water. They _____ **follow** the directions.	You _____ **use** hot water. They **must not miss** a step.

> Check your answers: Grammar reference, p. 111

7. Complete the sentences with the affirmative or negative of the words.

1. We __shouldn't put__ (should / put) metal in the microwave. It can start a fire.
2. Sara _____ (have to / wash) her clothes today. She can do it tomorrow.
3. I _____ (should / get) a small hair dryer for my trip. My suitcase only has room for small things.
4. Jack and Paula _____ (have to / buy) a new dishwasher. Theirs broke.
5. Don _____ (must / use) his vacuum cleaner before 8:00 p.m. His parents don't like noise late at night.

8. Complete the sentences with should (not), (not) have to, or must (not).

1. Jenny _____ get a lamp for her bedroom. It's really dark.
2. The label says, "You _____ put the hair dryer in water." You will get hurt.
3. I _____ set my alarm clock on Saturday because I don't work on the weekend!
4. We _____ make the vegetables in the microwave. They're better on the stove.
5. My sister _____ wash her clothes at the laundromat. She doesn't have a washing machine at home.

> **Get it RIGHT!**
>
> Use **must** for obligation, not for things that are responsibilities.
> You **have to bring** a pencil to class.
> (= It's your responsibility to bring a pencil.)
> You **must use** a pencil on the test.
> (= It's an obligation to use a pencil. You're not allowed to use a pen or a marker.)

Speaking: Guess the appliance

9. YOUR TURN Work with a partner. Think of an appliance. Describe it, and tell your partner how you should (not), (not) have to, must (not) use it. Your partner guesses the appliance. Take turns.

> It's small, and it's often white. You have to plug it in. You use it in the kitchen. You shouldn't put metal in it.

> Is it a microwave?

> Yes, it is!

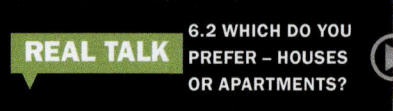

At Home

Conversation: I have to clean the house.

1. **REAL TALK** Watch or listen to the teenagers. Are these reasons for preferring houses or apartments? Write *H* (house) or *A* (apartment).

    1. ____ They're usually bigger.
    2. ____ They're quieter.
    3. ____ They usually have a garden.
    4. ____ They're usually closer to the center of a city.

> **NOTICE IT**
> Some words are different in American English and British English.
>
> | American English | British English |
> |---|---|
> | apartment | flat |
> | yard | garden |

2. **YOUR TURN** Which do *you* prefer – houses or apartments? Tell your partner. Give a reason for your answer.

3. Josh is helping Cara with her chores. Listen and complete the conversation.

USEFUL LANGUAGE: Asking for and offering help
- Can I ask you for a favor?
- Could you help me out?
- Would you like some help?
- I'll give you a hand.

Josh: Are you ready to go the mall?

Cara: I'm sorry, but I can't go yet. I didn't finish my chores. I have to clean **the living room**.

Josh: ¹_____

Cara: Oh, yes. That'd be great. I'll **clean the furniture**, and you can **vacuum**.

Josh: OK. Let's get started.

Cara: I need to get the cleaning supplies out of that cabinet. I can't reach them.

Josh: Wait. ²_____

Cara: Great, thanks.

Josh: Hey . . . ³_____

Cara: Of course.

Josh: I need to get a birthday present for my sister. ⁴_____

Cara: Sure. Let's finish cleaning **the living room** and then shop for your sister.

4. Practice the conversation with a partner.

5. **YOUR TURN** Repeat the conversation in Exercise 3, but change the words in **purple**. Use the information in the chart for one conversation and your own ideas for another.

		Your ideas
Room to clean	the kitchen	
Chore #1	clean the sink	
Chore #2	put the dishes in the dishwasher	

To santiagoG@middleschool.cup.org
From jorge.vegasrg@net.cup.org
Subject My House

Hi Santiago,

I'm excited you're coming to stay with us in our new house for the summer! We live in a big house with four bedrooms. My parents have the biggest bedroom, and they have their own bathroom. My sister and I have our own bedrooms. There's a fourth bedroom, but now it's my mom's office. My bedroom is pretty big. I have two beds, so you can sleep in my room. There's room for your clothes in my dresser.

Downstairs there's a big living room. We have a sofa, two armchairs, and a huge TV! My favorite room is the kitchen. There's a big table where we eat, talk, and play games. There's a dishwasher, so we don't have to wash dishes by hand!

Tell me about your apartment.

Your cousin,

Jorge

Reading to write: A description of Jorge's house

6. Look at the photo of Jorge's house. How many bedrooms do you think it has? Read the email to check.

> ◉ *Focus on* **CONTENT**
> When you write about your house, include:
> - the size, age, and kind of house
> - how many bedrooms it has
> - what other rooms it has
> - your favorite room and why
> - some of the furniture or appliances there

7. Read Jorge's email again. What information does he include for each category from the Focus on Content box?

> ◉ *Focus on* **LANGUAGE**
> **Commas**
> Use commas to separate items in a list.
> *I have a desk, two chairs, and big bed in my bedroom.*
> Use commas to join two complete sentences with conjunctions like *and*, *but*, and *so*.
> *We usually cook in the oven, but sometimes we use the microwave.*

8. Find examples in Jorge's email of the comma rules in the Focus on Language box.

9. Put commas in the correct places.
   1. My bedroom is small but it's comfortable.
   2. There are four chairs a big table and two lamps in our kitchen.
   3. The dishwasher isn't working so I have to wash the dishes by hand.
   4. I packed a hair dryer a toothbrush and shampoo in my suitcase.

Writing: An email about your house

◯ PLAN
Use the categories in the Focus on Content box and take notes about your home.

Size, age, and kind	
Number of bedrooms	
Other rooms	
Favorite room/why	
Furniture/appliances	

◯ WRITE
Write an email describing your house to a friend or someone in your family. Use your notes to help you. Write at least 80 words.

◯ CHECK
Check your writing. Can you answer "yes" to these questions?

- Is information for each category of the Focus on Content box in your description?
- Do you use commas correctly?

Workbook, pp. 40–41

LIFE ON THE WATER

Did you know that some people live on the water? You can find houseboats on lakes, rivers, and canals all over the world. There are hundreds in Sausalito, California. Thirteen-year-old Ryan Harvey moved to a houseboat community with his family two years ago. We asked Ryan about a typical Saturday on his houseboat.

7:00 A.M. WILDLIFE WATCH
Early morning is the best time to see marine animals because it's the quietest time of the day. Sometimes, I can see seals right outside my bedroom window. They're amazing!

5:00 P.M. VISIT FRIENDS
We often go out in our kayaks to see other families on their boats. I paddle faster than my parents!

10:15 A.M. MORNING WALK
I go with Dad to get our mail at the marina. It's where all our neighbors meet. I always see my friends there.

7:00 P.M. DINNER
Dad makes dinner, and we eat on the balcony on top of our houseboat when the weather is nice. Because we're far from the town, there aren't any streetlights. You can see the stars at night!

1:00 P.M. LUNCH
The kitchen is very small, so only one person fits. Mom and I take turns making lunch. I usually cook more slowly than my mom.

"There's not much room on the houseboat, but you're closer to nature. It's also safer and quieter than the city. I love life on the water!"

Culture: Living on a houseboat

1. Look at the photos. Do you think the boy is at home or on vacation?

2. Read and listen to the article. What are some advantages to living on a houseboat? What are some disadvantages?

3. Read the article again. Number the activities in order from 1–6.
   ___ Ryan's mom cooks.
   ___ Ryan's family eats outside.
   ___ Ryan sees animals.
   ___ Ryan's family goes out on the water.
   ___ Ryan's dad cooks.
   ___ Ryan and his dad go for a walk.

4. **YOUR TURN** Work with a partner. Would you like to live on a houseboat? Why or why not? What other kind of house would you like to live in?

   I'd like to live on a houseboat because . . . I'd also like to live . . .

   I wouldn't like to live on a houseboat because . . . I'd like to live . . .

BE CURIOUS Find out about someone who buys a house. Why does he want to move it? (Workbook, p. 83)

Discovery EDUCATION
6.3 MOVING HOUSE

62 | Unit 6

UNIT 6 REVIEW

Vocabulary

 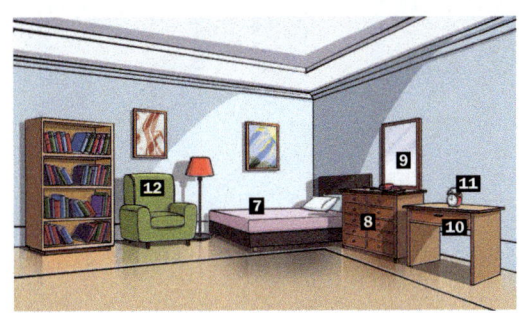

1. **Write the words for the furniture, items, and appliances next to the correct numbers.**

   1. _____   7. _____
   2. _____   8. _____
   3. _____   9. _____
   4. _____   10. _____
   5. _____   11. _____
   6. _____   12. _____

Grammar

2. **Write sentences with the comparative or superlative form of the adjectives and adverbs.**

   1. these tablets / be / good / those laptops

   _____
   _____

   2. Tara / have / comfortable / bed / in the house

   _____
   _____

   3. we usually / walk / far / our cousins

   _____
   _____

   4. my dog / bark / loudly / your dog

   _____
   _____

   5. the water / move / slowly / in the winter

   _____
   _____

3. **Circle the correct words.**

   1. Look at that sign. You **must not / don't have to** eat in the library.

   2. You **have to / shouldn't** turn off the computer before you leave. It can't stay on all night.

   3. You **don't have to / shouldn't** download any computer games onto the school computers. The teacher doesn't like it.

   4. You **should / don't have to** cook tonight. I'm going to make dinner.

   5. You **must / should** ask for help if you have a problem. It's a good idea.

Useful language

4. **Look at the underlined words in the conversations. Write A if the person is asking for help. Write O if the person is offering help.**

   1. ____
   A: The iron is up so high in that cabinet. I can't reach it.
   B: <u>Would you like some help?</u>
   A: Sure. That'd be great.

   2. ____
   A: I don't understand this recipe. <u>Could you help me out?</u>
   B: Sure. Let me see it.

   3. ____
   A: Hey, Sue. Do you want to go to a movie?
   B: Sure, but, <u>can I ask you for a favor</u> first?
   A: OK.

PROGRESS CHECK: Now I can . . .

☐ identify rooms in a house and household items.
☐ compare two or more rooms.
☐ identify and talk about household appliances.
☐ ask for and offer help.
☐ write an email about my house.
☐ talk about the kind of house I'd like to live in.

REVIEW UNITS 5–6, Workbook, pp. 42–43

7 VISIONS of the FUTURE

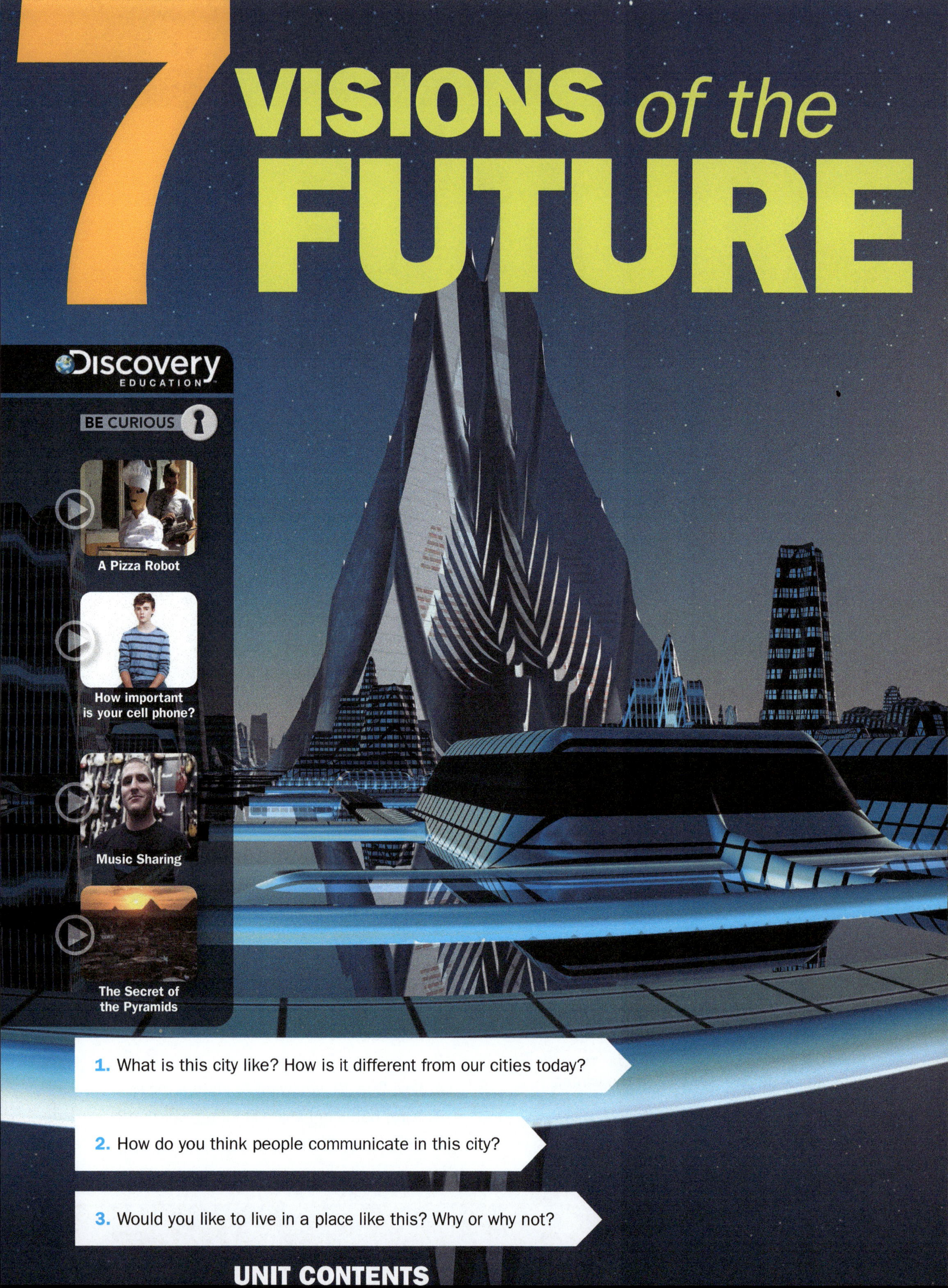

Discovery EDUCATION

BE CURIOUS

A Pizza Robot

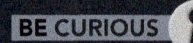
How important is your cell phone?

Music Sharing

The Secret of the Pyramids

1. What is this city like? How is it different from our cities today?

2. How do you think people communicate in this city?

3. Would you like to live in a place like this? Why or why not?

UNIT CONTENTS

Vocabulary Computers and communication; technology verbs
Grammar *Will* and *won't* for predictions; adverbs of possibility; first conditional with *will* (*not*), *may* (*not*), and *might* (*not*)
Listening They're always coming out with something new.

Vocabulary: Computers and communication

1. Match the words (a–i) with the correct pictures.

   a. a keyboard   d. a printer   g. a touch pad
   b. a flash drive   e. a smartphone   h. a touch screen
   c. a mouse   f. a tablet   ✓ i. Wi-Fi

1. *i*   2. ☐   3. ☐   4. ☐

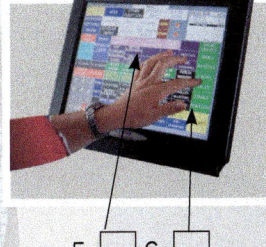   

5. ☐ 6. ☐   7. ☐   8. ☐   9. ☐

2. Listen, check, and repeat.

3. Circle the correct words.
   1. Do you usually use **Wi-Fi / a touch pad** or a mouse?
   2. You can save your work on **a flash drive / a touch pad**.
   3. You use **Wi-Fi / a printer** to go on the Internet.
   4. You use **a mouse / a keyboard** to type an email.
   5. You can carry **a smartphone / a touch screen** easily in one hand.
   6. I prefer **a flash drive / a mouse** to a touch pad.

Say it RIGHT!
The letters **ou** can sound like the /uh/ or /ow/ sound. Listen to the sentence.
My cousin has three computers in her house.
Which words in Exercise 1 have the letters **ou**? What sounds do they make?

Speaking: A computer quiz

4. **YOUR TURN** Use the words from Exercise 1 to give information about you.
   Something I use:
   • at school: _____
   • to do homework: _____
   • at home: _____
   • every day: _____
   • to play games: _____
   • to communicate with friends: _____

5. Work with a partner. Share your answers to the quiz in Exercise 4.

   > I use Wi-Fi, a printer, and a touch pad at school.

Workbook, p. 44

Reading Computers: A Big Past, A Small Future; How do you think people will listen to music in the future?; Television Grows Up . . . and Down!
Conversation Asking for and giving instructions
Writing An opinion paragraph

The Future of Technology

Computers: A Big Past, A Small Future

Over 65 years ago, the world's first computer was "born." Scientists called it "The Baby," but it was huge. It filled an entire room! Three people made the computer and programmed math problems for it. On June 19, 1948, the computer solved its first math problem – in 52 minutes! At that time, this was amazing.

Computers are now much smaller. With touch-screen technology, many computers don't need extra things, like a keyboard or a mouse. In the future, computers probably won't need these things at all. Some computers, like the smartphone, can fit in one hand. Computers are also more powerful today. There is more computing power in a smartphone than there was in all of the computers on *Apollo 11*, the first spacecraft to take people to the moon!

How else will computers change in the future? A computer's "brain" is a chip inside the computer, and in the future, people will definitely be able to save much more information on a computer chip. So, computers will be smaller and even more powerful. Perhaps they'll even think like humans! Maybe we won't need to tell computers what to do because they'll decide for themselves!

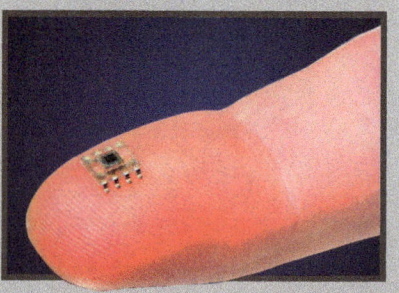

Reading: An article about computers

1. Work with a partner. Look at the photo of an old computer. How was it different from modern computers?

 2. Read and listen to the article. What was the first computer like?

3. Read the article again. Circle the correct answers.

   1. The first computer fit in _____.
      a. a hand   b. a room   c. a building
   2. The Baby found the answer to _____ math problem(s) in 52 minutes.
      a. 1   b. 3   c. 65
   3. The computers on *Apollo 11* were _____ a smartphone.
      a. more powerful than   b. less powerful than   c. as powerful as
   4. Today, many computers don't have _____.
      a. keyboards   b. chips   c. touch screens

4. **YOUR TURN** Work with a partner. Think of at least five things you think computers should do in the future.

   > Computers should clean our houses in the future. They should . . .

5. **YOUR TURN** Join another pair. Share your ideas from Exercise 4. Which idea do you think is the best?

DID YOU KNOW...?

There are more than two billion personal computers in the world today, including tablets and smartphones.

Grammar: *will* and *won't* for predictions

6. Complete the chart.

Use *will* and *won't* to predict future events.		
Wh- questions	**Affirmative answers**	**Negative answers**
What **will** my smartphone **do** in the future?	Perhaps it**'ll think** like a human.	It _____ **drive** a car.
How _____ computers **change**?	They _____ **be** smaller.	They **won't be** bigger.
Yes/No questions	**Short answers**	
_____ my smartphone **think** like a human?	Yes, it **will**.	No, it _____.
Will computers **change**?	Yes, they _____.	No, they **won't**.
Contractions: I will = I**'ll** you will = you**'ll** he will = he**'ll** she will = she**'ll** it will = _____ we will = we**'ll** they will = _____		

> Check your answers: Grammar reference, p. 112

7. In 1900, an American engineer made these predictions. Complete them with *will* or *won't* and the correct verbs.

buy   eat   not be   not cook   ✓ not live   not wait   talk

1. Animals __won't live__ in the wild.
2. People _____ on wireless phones.
3. We _____ all of our own meals. We _____ them in stores.
4. The letters C, X, and Q _____ in the alphabet.
5. We _____ until summer to eat vegetables. We _____ them in winter.

8. Work with a partner. Which predictions in Exercise 7 are true now?

9. Write sentences about the future with *will* and *won't*. How sure are you? Use *definitely, certainly, probably, maybe,* or *perhaps*.

1. we / have / Wi-Fi connections in our clothes
   We'll probably have Wi-Fi connections in our clothes.
2. cars / not need / human drivers
   _____
3. people / live / to be 120 years old
   _____
4. we / not use / pens and pencils
   _____

Adverbs of possibility		
Sure	**Pretty sure**	**Not as sure**
definitely certainly	probably	maybe perhaps
Use adverbs of possibility to say how sure you are about a prediction. **Definitely**, **certainly**, and **probably** come between the subject and **will** or **won't**, or between **will** and the base form of the verb. **Perhaps** and **maybe** come before the subject.		
They **definitely** will think like humans.		
They'll **probably** think like humans.		
Perhaps they will think like humans.		

Speaking: Predictions about my future

10. YOUR TURN Work with a partner. Ask and answer questions about the future. Make predictions about the items below or your own ideas.

your school/job   your friends/family   your town/city   your computer

> What will you do in the future?

> I'll probably write software for computers.

Find out about a new technology. How do the people get pizza? (Workbook, p. 84)

7.1 A PIZZA ROBOT

Using TECHNOLOGY

Listening: They're always coming out with something new.

1. Do you and your friends play video games? What do you play?

2. Listen to Jenna and Karl talk about a video game. Who wants to work with computers in the future?

3. Listen again. Are the sentences true (*T*) or false (*F*)?
    1. Karl has a new game console. ___
    2. There aren't any boy characters in Cyber Chase. ___
    3. Jenna and Karl play Ocean World. ___
    4. Jenna wants a game console for her birthday. ___
    5. Karl thinks Jenna should get a Ztron 2100. ___
    6. Karl is taking a computer class. ___

Vocabulary: Technology verbs

4. Match the pictures with the correct sentences. Then listen and check your answers.

    1. _c_ To see the bottom of the web page, **scroll down**. To go back to the top, **scroll up**.
    2. ___ **Click on** the item you want.
    3. ___ To see more of the city on the map, **zoom out**. To look at your street, **zoom in**.
    4. ___ You can **sign into** your web page from any computer. Don't forget to **sign out** when you're done!
    5. ___ Do you **shut down** your computer at night?
    6. ___ **Turn on** your computer with the power button.
    7. ___ I **back up** my files every day.

5. **YOUR TURN** Work with a partner. Tell your partner how to do one of these things on a computer. Use the phrases in Exercise 4.

listen to music	read a blog	watch a video	write an email

    > Turn on your computer. Then sign into your email account. Next, . . .

68 | Unit 7

Grammar: First conditional with will (not), may (not), and might (not)

6. Complete the chart.

Use the first conditional to show results or possible results of future actions. Use *if* and the simple present in the main clause and **will** (not), **may** (not), or **might** (not) and the base form of a verb in the result clause.
Statements
You'**ll see** all of the choices **if** you **zoom out**.
If I **make** games, they **won't be** boring.
_____ I **ask** my parents, they **might get** it for me for my birthday.
I **may not get** the Ztron 2100 _____ a newer model **comes** out.
Questions
What kind of games _____ you **make if** you'**re** a designer?   Action games.
If I **beat** you, **will** you **do** my homework?   Yes, I **will**. / No, I _____.

> **NOTICE IT**
> The *if* clause can come at the beginning or end of the sentence. Use a comma after the *if* clause when it comes at the beginning.
> *If you scroll down,* you'll see more characters.
> You'll see more characters *if you scroll down.*

Check your answers: Grammar reference, p. 112

7. Circle the correct words.

1. If Joe **learns** / **might learn** to write code, he **gets** / **might get** a great tech job.
2. If my parents **get** / **will get** a new computer, they **don't buy** / **won't buy** a tablet.
3. You **don't lose** / **won't lose** your files if you **back** / **may back** them up.
4. I **buy** / **may buy** a new smartphone if I **get** / **will get** enough money for my birthday.
5. **Will I get** / **Do I get** to your blog if I **click on** / **will click on** this link?
6. If my computer **stops** / **will stop** working, I **don't finish** / **may not finish** my homework.
7. If you **decide** / **will decide** to get a printer, which one **do you buy** / **will you buy**?
8. Your tablet **shuts down** / **will shut down** if you **click on** / **will click on** that.

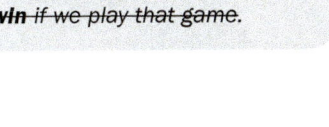

> **Get it RIGHT!**
> Do not use the simple present in the main clause with the first conditional.
> *I'll win* if we play that game.
> NOT: ~~I win if we play that game.~~

8. Complete the paragraph with the simple present or *will* (not).

If I ¹ _pass_ (pass) all of my exams, my parents ² _____ (buy) me a new tablet. If I ³ _____ (get) a new tablet, I ⁴ _____ (start) my own website. I ⁵ _____ (post) a video of my dog riding a skateboard if I ⁶ _____ (make) my own website. If one million people ⁷ _____ (like) my video, I ⁸ _____ (be) famous! I ⁹ _____ (not be) famous if no one ¹⁰ _____ (watch) my video. If I ¹¹ _____ (fail) any of my exams, my parents ¹² _____ (not buy) me a tablet. I should start studying!

Speaking: A lot of *Ifs*!

9. YOUR TURN Ask and answer questions with the ideas below or your own ideas. Use *will* (not), *may* (not), or *might* (not).

> If I have a website in the future, . . .   If I buy a computer in the future, . . .
> If I make a video in the future, . . .

> What will you post if you have a website in the future?

> If I have a website, I'll post funny videos.

Workbook, pp. 46–47

 REAL TALK 7.2 HOW IMPORTANT IS YOUR CELL PHONE?

Tech TRENDS

Conversation: Using your cell phone

1. **REAL TALK** Watch or listen to the teenagers. How many think their cell phones are important? How many don't think they're important? Write the numbers.

Important	Not important

2. **YOUR TURN** How important is *your* cell phone? Tell your partner.

3. Kendra is telling her grandmother how to make a call on a smartphone. Listen and complete the conversation.

USEFUL LANGUAGE: Asking for and giving instructions

you need to | all you have to | how do I | How does it work?

Grandma: Can I borrow your phone to **call Grandpa**?
Kendra: Sure. Here's my smartphone.
Grandma: ¹_____
Kendra: First, ²_____ press the round button to turn it on.
Grandma: Like this?
Kendra: Yes. That's it. See . . . it's a touch screen. Now, click on the **phone** icon.
Grandma: OK. So, ³_____ **make a call**?
Kendra: **Click on the contacts icon and scroll down to Grandpa's name.**
Grandma: OK. Now what?
Kendra: ⁴_____ do is **click on his name**.
Grandma: I see. That was easy!

4. Practice the conversation with a partner.

5. **YOUR TURN** Repeat the conversation in Exercise 3, but change the words in purple. Use the information in the chart for one conversation and your own ideas for another.

		My ideas
Task	text Aunt Linda	
Type of icon	text message	
Task	send a text	
Step 1	scroll down to Aunt Linda's name and click on it	
Step 2	type your text and click on "send"	

70 | Unit 7

TechIt Question of the Week:

How do you think people will listen to music in the future? Marcus Howard   posted 10/18

In my opinion, people will listen to music from computer chips in their clothing. One reason is that it will be an easy way to listen to music. People won't need to carry MP3 players or even smartphones for music. Small computer chips will be in sunglasses, hats, jackets, and shirts. Another reason is that some of this technology exists already. For example, you can buy sunglasses that play music. If this trend continues, it will be popular in the future. In conclusion, I think people will listen to music in their clothing, and it will be great!

👍 2   👎 0

Reading to write: An opinion paragraph

6. Look at the title and the photo. How does Marcus think people will listen to music in the future? Read his paragraph to check.

Focus on CONTENT
In an opinion paragraph, include:
- **A** an introduction to the topic and your opinion
- **B** reasons for your opinion
- **C** facts and examples to support your reasons
- **D** a conclusion with your opinion

7. Read Marcus's paragraph again. Label the sentences in the paragraph with the items in the Focus on Content box (A–D).

Focus on LANGUAGE
You can use these phrases in opinion pieces:
To give opinions: **In my opinion,**   **I think (that)**
                  I believe (that)
To give reasons: **One reason**   **Another reason**
                  is (that)   **is (that)**
To conclude: **In conclusion,**   **For these reasons,**

8. Find examples of the phrases in the Focus on Language box in Marcus's paragraph.

9. Complete the paragraph.

| another reason is that | I believe that | one reason is that |
| for these reasons | in my opinion | |

¹_____, people will ride in cars without **drivers** in the future. ²_____ it will make streets **safer**. The cars will drive themselves with new technology. If **people** don't drive, accidents won't happen. ³_____ it will save people a lot of money. The cars will be electric, and people won't have to buy gas. ⁴_____ this will happen because the technology already exists. ⁵_____, people won't drive cars in the future.

Writing: Your opinion paragraph

PLAN
Choose one of the topics about the future or your own idea. Write notes about it.

How do you think people will . . . in the future?

communicate with each other	listen to music
read books	shop
travel	use their smartphones

Topic and opinion: _____

Reason	Fact / Example

WRITE
Write an opinion paragraph about your topic. Use your notes to help you. Write at least 80 words.

CHECK
Check your writing. Can you answer "yes" to these questions?

- Is information for each category from the Focus on Content box in your paragraph?
- Do you use the expressions from the Focus on Language box correctly?

Workbook, pp. 48–49

Television Grows Up... and Down!

People in every country and every culture watch television. You watch TV differently than your parents and grandparents did. And TV watching will probably be different in the future.

The story of TV started over 80 years ago. In 1936, there were only about 200 televisions. Sixty years later, there were one billion TVs worldwide. The first TVs were big, square boxes, and the TV shows were in black and white. People had to get off the couch to turn on the TV and change the channel with a button on the front of the TV. Color TVs arrived in the 1950s. Today, all TVs are in color, and people change the channel with remote controls. And there are more channels. When TV started, there were only a few channels, and now there are hundreds!

In 1973, the first big-screen TV was in stores. Today, TVs are getting bigger – and smaller. People have huge flat-screen TVs, and some have surround sound. It's like being at a movie theater at home. "TVs" are also getting smaller. Many people watch TV shows on their tablets and smartphones. Some shows are only available online.

How will people watch TV in the future? Some newer inventions are 3D television and smart TVs with Wi-Fi connections. Some people say our TVs at home will get even bigger, while the gadgets we watch TV on will get smaller; for example, there are "TV watches" and "TV glasses." Most people agree that TV watching will definitely stay popular.

DID YOU KNOW...?
The remote control arrived in 1956. Surround sound, sound that comes from speakers instead of just the TV, was first available for TVs in 1982.

Culture: How we watch TV

7.08

1. **Look at the photos. How are TVs today different than they were in the past?**

2. **Read and listen to the article. What is the main idea?**
   a. how we watch TV today
   b. the history of TV watching
   c. the future of TV watching

3. **Read the article again. Are the sentences true or false? Write *T* (true), *F* (false), or *NI* (no information).**
   1. The first TVs were in color and black and white. ___
   2. In 1996, there were about one billion TVs in the world. ___
   3. Today, there are over 500 TV channels. ___
   4. Big TVs aren't popular today because people watch shows on their phones. ___
   5. There are some shows you can only watch online. ___
   6. In the future, everyone will watch 3D TV shows. ___

4. **YOUR TURN** Work with a partner. How do you watch TV now? How do you think you'll watch TV in the future?

Workbook, p. 85

BE CURIOUS Find out about Napster. What is it? (Workbook, p. 85)

Discovery EDUCATION
7.3 MUSIC SHARING

UNIT 7 REVIEW

Vocabulary

1. Label the photos with the correct words.

1. _____ 3. _____

2. _____ 4. _____

2. Circle the correct words.

   1. How often do you **scroll up / back up** your files?
   2. If you **zoom in / sign into**, you can see my house on the map.
   3. Will you please **turn on / shut down** my computer when you're done with it?
   4. **Click on / Zoom out** that link to see the photos I posted.

Grammar

3. Write sentences about the future with *will* or *won't* and the word in parentheses.

   1. Everyone works at home. (probably)

      Everyone will probably work at home.

   2. People have robots in their houses. (perhaps)

      _____

   3. Students don't use flash drives. (definitely)

      _____

   4. We go to the moon for vacation. (maybe)

      _____

4. Match the phrases to make sentences.

   1. If you're going to be late, ___
   2. If you get a smaller computer, ___
   3. If I don't study tonight, ___
   4. What will you do ___

   a. if your computer breaks?
   b. I won't pass my test tomorrow.
   c. will you send me a text message?
   d. it will be easier to carry.

Useful language

5. Circle the correct answers.

   1. **A:** This is a great new video game.
      B: How does it **work / need / do**?
   2. **A:** **What / How / Who** do I send an email from my phone?
      B: First, sign into your email account.
   3. **A:** Can you help me download this app?
      B: Sure. First, you **need to / click on / will to** go to the app store.
   4. **A:** How do I shut down my tablet?
      B: All you **like to / don't have to / have to** do is hold that button down for a few seconds.

PROGRESS CHECK: Now I can . . .

- ☐ talk about computers and technology.
- ☐ make predictions about the future.
- ☐ talk about how to use technology.
- ☐ ask for and give instructions.
- ☐ write an opinion paragraph.
- ☐ talk about how I watch TV today and in the future.

CLIL PROJECT

7.4 The Secret of the Pyramids, p. 119

8 The CHOICES We MAKE

BE CURIOUS

A School at Home

What are you going to do when you leave school?

Time for an Adventure!

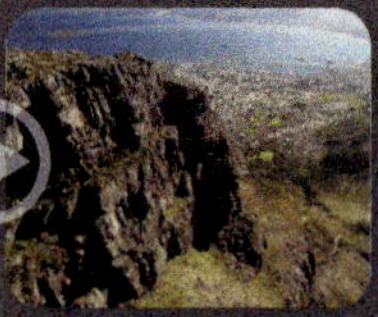

1. What decision do you think this person has to make?

2. What decisions do you have to make in your life?

3. What do you do when you have to make a difficult decision?

UNIT CONTENTS
Vocabulary Life events; containers and materials
Grammar *be going to* and *will*; present continuous and simple present for future
Listening An eco-project

Vocabulary: Life events

1. Match the pictures (a–j) with the correct words and phrases.

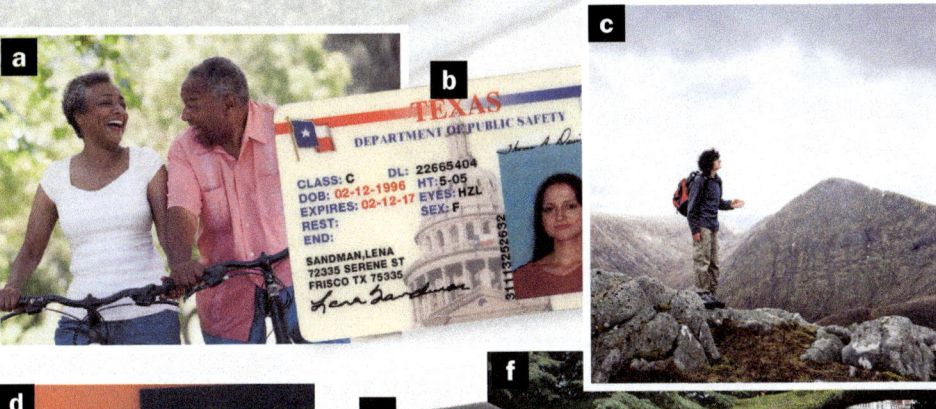

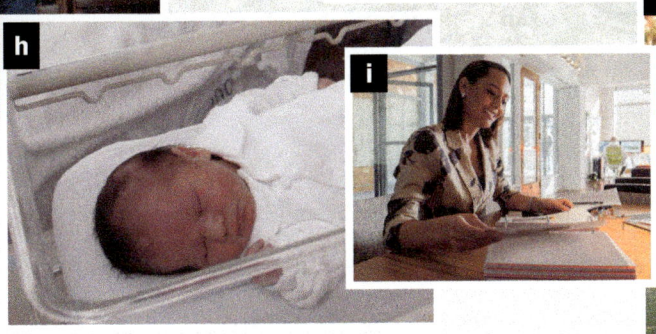

1. _h_ be born
2. ___ finish school
3. ___ get a job
4. ___ get married
5. ___ get your driver's license
6. ___ go to college
7. ___ go to school
8. ___ have children
9. ___ retire
10. ___ take a year off

 2. Listen, check, and repeat.

3. In which order do people usually do the life events in Exercise 1?

> First, people are born. Then they go to school. After that . . .

Speaking: About someone's life

4. **YOUR TURN** Work with a partner. Tell your partner about a parent's life or the life of another relative or adult you know. What do they have in common?

> My mother was born in 1967. She went to school in Durango, Mexico. She went to college at the University of Texas. After college, she got a job at . . .

> My Uncle Jim was born in 1967, too. But he went to school in . . .

 Workbook, p. 50

Reading Life in the Outback; Farah's Application Letter; A Summer in Alaska
Conversation Agreeing and disagreeing
Writing An application letter

UNUSUAL LIVES

Life in the Outback

by Lauren Birch

The outback is a large area in the middle of Australia. Not many people live there, and most of them are sheep farmers. Matt Clark lives on a "sheep station" with his parents and sister. I interviewed Matt to find out about life in the outback.

Q: Do you work?

A: Yes. I help my parents on the farm and take care of the sheep. It's very hard, but I love it!

Q: Where do you go to school?

A: My sister and I go to the "school of the air." We have classes with other kids and a teacher on our computer. We can see and hear each other with web cams. We take quizzes and tests online, and we also email homework to our teacher.

Q: How do you see friends?

A: My friends live far away, but we're lucky because my family has a small airplane. We fly to the nearest town every month to see friends and go shopping. My school has special events, too. I'm going to go to a camp next month!

Q: What are you going to do after you finish school? Will you stay on the farm?

A: I'm going to study agriculture in college in Sydney. But I think I'll come back here to live. I was born here, and this is my home.

DID YOU KNOW...?
About 60,000 people live in the outback, and there are over 70 million sheep!

Reading: An interview about life in the outback

1. Look at the photos. Where do you think it is? Would you want to live there?

2. Read and listen to the article. Why does the reporter interview Matt?

   a. to find out about an unusual school

   b. to find out about life on a sheep farm

   c. to find out about his college plans

3. Read the article again. Are the sentences true (*T*) or false (*F*)? Correct the false sentences.

   1. Most Australians live in the center of Australia. ___
   2. Matt works with his parents. ___
   3. Matt flies in a plane to get to school. ___
   4. Matt's friends don't live near his sheep station. ___
   5. Matt's family goes to a town every week. ___
   6. Matt plans to leave his home and return in the future. ___

4. **YOUR TURN** Work with a partner. Answer the questions.

   1. How is Matt's life different from your life?

      > Matt's life is different from mine because he has to work, and . . .

   2. What do you think are the positive and negative things about life in the outback?

      > One positive thing is . . .

Grammar: *be going to* and *will*

5. Complete the chart.

Use *be going to* to talk about plans in the future.
Use *will* to talk about predictions and unplanned decisions.

be going to	will
Wh- questions and answers	
What **are** you **going to do**?	Where **will** he **live**?
I'm _____ study agriculture.	He**'ll live** in the outback.
I**'m not going to study** history.	He _____ **live** in Sydney.
Yes/No questions and answers	
Is he **going to study** history?	_____ you **stay** here?
Yes, he _____. / No, he **isn't**.	Yes, I **will**. / No, I **won't**.

> Check your answers: Grammar reference, p. 113

 Say it RIGHT!

The *i* in *will* is a short *i* (/ɪ/), and the *e* in *we'll* is a long *e* (/e/). However, in speaking, *will* and *we'll* often sound alike. They both can sound like /wɪl/. Listen to the sentences.
I wɪll get married to Tom next year.
We'll get married in May.
Ask and answer the questions in Exercise 6 with a partner. Pay attention to the pronunciation of *will* and *we'll*.

6. Match the questions with the answers.

1. _e_ Will Sheila retire next year?
2. ___ When are you going to go to college?
3. ___ Will you get your driver's licenses in June?
4. ___ Are Tom and Rita getting married next month?
5. ___ When will you finish school?
6. ___ Is Lily going to have children?

a. No, they're not.
b. Yes, she is.
c. I'm going to start in September.
d. We'll be done in a year.
e. Yes, she will.
f. No, we won't. We'll get them in July.

7. Complete the conversation with the correct form of *be going to* for future plans or *will* for predictions and unplanned decisions.

Mom: I'm worried about Neil.
Dad: Why? What's the problem?
Mom: He says he ¹ *is going to get* (get) an after-school job.
Dad: That ² _____ (be) really difficult! ³ _____ he _____ (stop) playing soccer?
Mom: No, he ⁴ _____ (stay) on the team.
Dad: When ⁵ _____ he _____ (study)?
Mom: I don't know. I don't think he should get a job until the summer.
Dad: I agree! Maybe he ⁶ _____ (change) his mind. I ⁷ _____ (talk) to him tonight.
Mom: You can try, but he probably ⁸ _____ (not listen) to you.

Speaking: Future plans and predictions

8. **YOUR TURN** Work with a partner. First, tell your partner about what you are going to do or not going to do in the future. Then give predictions about what you will or won't do.

> I'm going to take a year off when I finish school. I'm not going to start college right away. I think I'll go to Brazil. I'll probably go to the rain forest. I don't think I'll go to Rio . . . .

NOTICE IT

Think, *probably*, and *maybe* are often used with *will* for predictions and unplanned events.
He **thinks** he**'ll live** in the outback.
He **probably won't live** in Sydney.
Maybe they**'ll get** married next year.

 Find out about children who are homeschooled. What are some subjects they study? (Workbook, p. 86)

8.1 A SCHOOL AT HOME

Cleaning UP

Listening: An eco-project

1. Do you know anyone who took a year off after finishing high school? What did he or she do?

2. Listen to Olivia tell Dan about her sister's plans for a year off. What are her sister's plans?

3. Listen again. Circle the correct answers.
   1. Olivia's sister is going to _____.
      a. Costa Rica   b. Europe
   2. She's going to _____.
      a. help sea turtles   b. pick up trash
   3. She'll probably work in _____.
      a. a surf shop   b. a restaurant
   4. Olivia wants to _____ after she finishes high school.
      a. travel in Europe   b. work in Paris
   5. Dan wants to work _____ before he goes to college.
      a. on an eco-project   b. at home

Vocabulary: Containers and materials

4. Look at the pictures. Write the phrases next to the correct numbers. Then listen and check your answers.

| a cardboard box | a glass bottle | a metal can | a plastic bottle |
| a cloth bag | ✓ a glass jar | a paper bag | a plastic carton |

1. _a glass jar_
2. _____
3. _____
4. _____
5. _____
6. _____
7. _____
8. _____

5. Work with a partner. Answer the questions.
   1. What things come in the containers in Exercise 4?

   > Peanut butter comes in a glass jar or a plastic jar.

   > Pasta sauce does, too.

   2. Do you recycle containers in your home? What do you recycle?

   > In my home, we recycle . . .

Grammar: Present continuous and simple present for future

6. Complete the chart.

Present continuous	Simple present
As with **be going to**, *use the present continuous to talk about future plans. Use the simple present to talk about scheduled future events.*	
Wh- questions and answers	
Why _____ she **going** there?	When _____ she **start** the project?
She**'s taking** a year off.	She **starts** next week.
She**'s not traveling**.	She **doesn't start** tomorrow.
Yes/No questions and answers	
_____ they **helping** the turtles?	**Does** class **start** in five minutes?
Yes, they **are**. / No, they _____.	Yes, it _____. / No, it **doesn't**.

> Check your answers: Grammar reference, p. 113

7. Complete the sentences with the present continuous or simple present.

I ¹ *'m going* (go) to a class at the recycling center next week. The class ² _____ (be) on Tuesday. It ³ _____ (start) at 10:00 a.m., and it ⁴ _____ (end) at 4:00 p.m. My friend Vic ⁵ _____ (take) the class with me. We ⁶ _____ (not drive) to the recycling center. We ⁷ _____ (walk). Two people ⁸ _____ (teach) how to make chairs out of recycled cardboard boxes. I ⁹ _____ (not collect) boxes for the class because the recycling center ¹⁰ _____ (provide) the boxes next week.

> **Get it RIGHT!**
> Use the present continuous, not **will**, to talk about future arrangements.
> **I'm going** to Italy on July 15.
> NOT: ~~I'll go to Italy on July 15.~~

8. Correct the mistakes in the underlined words.

1. My roommate and I <u>recycle</u> our metal cans tomorrow.
2. The class <u>started</u> at 8:00 a.m. tomorrow.
3. I'm excited because I<u>'ll volunteer</u> at a recycling center next month.
4. We <u>are having</u> a meeting for the eco-project at 11:00 next Tuesday.
5. My sister and I <u>will go</u> to Costa Rica on May 10.

Speaking: Reuse it!

9. YOUR TURN Choose a container from the Vocabulary on page 78, and think of something you can make out of it. Then plan a class to teach people how to make the object. Fill out the chart.

Type of container	
What you will make	
Date of the class	
Where the class is	
When the class will start	
When the class will end	

10. Work with a partner. Tell your partner about your class. Your partner asks questions.

> In my class, I'm teaching people how to make flower vases out of plastic bottles.

> How many vases are you making?

Workbook, pp. 52–53

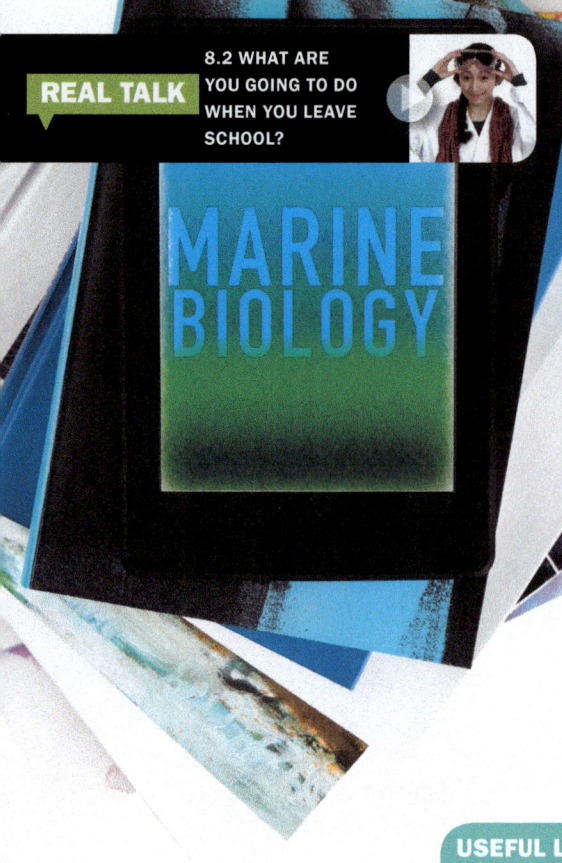

REAL TALK 8.2 WHAT ARE YOU GOING TO DO WHEN YOU LEAVE SCHOOL?

Our FUTURES

Conversation: I'm going to get a degree.

1. **REAL TALK** Watch or listen to the teenagers. Check (✓) the things they are going to do when they leave school.

   ☐ be the leader of a country ☐ play a sport
   ☐ buy something ☐ study a language
   ☐ get a driver's license ☐ visit someone
   ☐ have children ☐ volunteer somewhere
   ☐ marry someone ☐ work

2. **YOUR TURN** What are *you* going to do when you leave school? Tell your partner.

3. Listen to Lenny and Katie talking about their plans for when they finish school. Complete the conversation.

USEFUL LANGUAGE: Agreeing and disagreeing

Absolutely! | I disagree | I suppose you're right. | Maybe, but I think

Katie: I can't believe we'll finish school **in two years**! What are you going to do then?
Lenny: I'm definitely going to college.
Katie: What are you going to study?
Lenny: I think I'll study **marine biology**!
Katie: Wow! That's going to be difficult.
Lenny: ¹_____ I'll love the **science** classes, so it won't be too hard. What about you?
Katie: I'm going to take a year off. I want to volunteer at **a recycling center**. I think it's important.
Lenny: ²_____ Not enough people care about helping **the environment**.
Katie: Well, ³_____. A lot of people do things to help **the environment**.
Lenny: ⁴_____

4. Practice the conversation with a partner.

5. **YOUR TURN** Repeat the conversation in Exercise 3, but change the words in purple. Use the information in the chart for one conversation and your own ideas for another.

		Your ideas
Finish school	in May	
Subject to study	engineering	
Type of classes	math	
Where to volunteer	an animal shelter	
Who/What to help	animals	

80 | Unit 8

To: Morton@net.cup.org
From: FarahA@net.cup.org
Subject: Application letter

Dear Mr. Morton:

I am interested in volunteering at Clinton Hospital this summer. One day, I want to be a doctor and get a job in a hospital. I'm going to college in the fall, and I'm going to study medicine.

I'd like to help sick people. My mother was sick last year, and she had wonderful doctors. This inspired me to become a doctor. I want to help people have healthier lives.

For these reasons, I'd like to volunteer at your hospital. I'd work in any area, but I'd rather work with patients. Thank you for considering me for this volunteer position.

Sincerely,
Farah Ajam

Reading to write: An application letter

6. Look at the photo of Farah. What kind of job do you think she wants in the future? Read the email to check.

> ### Focus on CONTENT
> When you write an application letter, include this information:
> - **1** The position you're interested in
> - **2** Your long-term goals
> - **3** Your motivation for wanting the position
> - **4** Repeat the position you're interested in
> - **5** Thank the person you're writing to

7. Read Farah's letter again. What information does she include for each step in the Focus on Content box? Write the numbers by the sentences.

> ### Focus on LANGUAGE
> **want, would like ('d like), would rather ('d rather)**
> Use the infinitive form of a verb after **want** and **would like** to talk about things you want in the future.
> - He **wants to be** a scientist. He**'d like to work** with animals.
>
> Use the base form of a verb after **would rather** to talk about a preference.
> - I don't want to work in a hospital. **I'd rather work** in a doctor's office.
> - **I'd rather work** in a doctor's office **than** in a hospital.

8. Find examples in Farah's letter of the expressions in the Focus on Language box.

9. Complete the sentences with the infinitive or base form of the verbs.

1. Dina and Marcos want _____ (get) married in the spring.
2. I'd rather _____ (use) these cardboard boxes than throw them away.
3. Jenny would like _____ (retire) at age 60.
4. We don't want _____ (go) to college right away. We'd rather _____ (take) a year off first.
5. I'd like _____ (help) people learn about recycling.

 Writing: Your application letter

PLAN
First, think about a volunteer position that interests you. Choose one of these volunteer opportunities or use your own idea. Take notes.

a day-care center	a park
a library	a sea turtle program
a recycling center	

The position: _____

Your long-term goals	Your motivation
_____	_____
_____	_____
_____	_____

WRITE
Write an application letter for the volunteer opportunity. Use your notes to help you. Write at least 80 words.

CHECK
Check your writing. Can you answer "yes" to these questions?

- Is information for each category from the Focus on Content box in your letter?
- Do you use *want*, *would like*, and *would rather* correctly?

A SUMMER IN ALASKA

Do you have summer plans? Are you looking for an interesting experience? Then do something different and discover Alaska. We organize summer activities for young people. Help others and gain experience in a possible future career! Here are our three most popular programs.

A MARINE VOLUNTEER
Work with professional ocean scientists at an aquarium and wildlife rescue center. You'll learn about octopuses, sea lions, and other ocean animals. You'll learn from the scientists as they study these animals. Volunteers help with research and animal rescue, and they teach others about marine life. This is a great first step to a career in marine biology!

B PARK VOLUNTEER
Work in one of the many parks in Alaska. You'll stay in a cabin right in the park and use public showers and a dining room near your cabin. You'll help keep the park clean, and you'll learn a lot about Alaska's wild animals, like bears and moose. Many volunteers will take park visitors on hikes and tell them about Alaska's plants and animals. This is an excellent experience for people interested in a job in conservation.

C COMMUNITY VOLUNTEER
Work and live in a local Alaskan community. You can work at a school and help children with their schoolwork and teach them computer skills. You'll even have the chance to start your own program. For example, you could start a recycling program or an afterschool club. You'll teach others, and you'll also learn about life in the community. It is a good experience for people interested in a teaching career.

Culture: Volunteer programs in Alaska

1. Look at the photos of volunteer activities in Alaska. What do you see? What do you think the volunteers do for each job?

2. Read and listen to the article. Match the volunteer programs in the article (A–C) with the future careers (1–3).
   1. a conservationist ___
   2. a teacher ___
   3. a marine biologist ___

3. Read the article again. Answer the questions.
   1. Who are the volunteer projects for? ___
   2. Where do park volunteers live? ___
   3. In which program can you start your own project? ___
   4. Which programs involve animals? ___
   5. Which programs involve teaching others? ___

4. **YOUR TURN** Work with a partner. Which place would you like to volunteer? Why? Do you know of any similar projects in your city or country?

   > I'd like to volunteer at a park because I love nature.
   >
   > In my country, there's a...

DID YOU KNOW...?
Some high schools in the United States, Canada, and other countries require students to do volunteer work before they finish school.

BE CURIOUS Find out about someone who wants to have an adventure. What are some things she might do? (Workbook, p. 87)

Discovery EDUCATION
8.3 TIME FOR AN ADVENTURE!

UNIT 8 REVIEW

Vocabulary

1. Complete the sentences with the words and phrases.

finish school	get a job
get a driver's license	go to college

1. My sister is going to _____ in Boston next year.
2. You have to take a test before you can _____ and have a car.
3. Amy would like to _____ at a computer design company.
4. I'll _____ in May. Then I'm going to work during the summer.

2. Complete the name of each container and the material it is made from.

1. M _ _ _ _ C _ _   2. P _ _ _ _ B _ _

3. G _ _ _ _ J _ _   4. C _ _ _ _ B _ _

Grammar

3. Circle *be going to* for future plans or *will* for predictions.

Mark: What ¹**will you / are you going to** do this summer?

Jenny: My cousin from Canada ²**will / is going to** visit us in June, and we ³**will / are going to** go on a trip to the mountains.

Mark: Do you think you'll go hiking?

Jenny: Yes, we ⁴**will / are**.

Mark: That sounds nice. I think it ⁵**will / is going to** be fun.

Jenny: Yeah, I know we ⁶**will / are going to** have a good time.

4. Write sentences. Use the present continuous or simple present.

1. we / go / to a restaurant / tonight
   _____
2. the volunteer program / start / on June 15
   _____
3. the recycling center / close / at 10:00 p.m. tonight
   _____
4. they / get married / in April
   _____

Useful language

5. Circle the correct answers.

1. **A:** I think it's a good idea to volunteer somewhere before college.
   B: I suppose you're _____. It's a great experience.
   a. right   b. true   c. false

2. **A:** That table made of plastic bottles is cool.
   B: _____. I think it's sort of ugly.
   a. I agree   b. I disagree   c. Absolutely

3. **A:** People should retire when they're 60.
   B: _____, but I think some people like to keep working, and that's OK, too.
   a. I disagree   b. Never   c. Maybe

4. **A:** I think everyone should recycle plastic, paper, and glass.
   B: _____!
   a. Absolutely   b. Never   c. Not now

PROGRESS CHECK: Now I can . . .

☐ identify and talk about life events.
☐ discuss future plans and predictions.
☐ talk about future plans and scheduled events.
☐ agree and disagree with someone.
☐ write an application letter.
☐ talk about places I'd like to volunteer.

REVIEW UNITS 7–8, Workbook, pp. 56–57

9 Watch OUT!

Discovery EDUCATION

BE CURIOUS

Danger in Our Food

Have you ever had an accident?

A Deadly Job

1. What is the teen going to do?
2. Why do you think this is exciting? Do you think it's dangerous?
3. What exciting activities do you or your friends do?

UNIT CONTENTS

Vocabulary Accident and injury verbs; parts of the body
Grammar Present perfect statements with regular and irregular verbs; present perfect questions; present perfect vs. simple past
Listening I'm accident-prone.

Vocabulary: Accident and injury verbs

1. Complete the sentences with the words in the box.

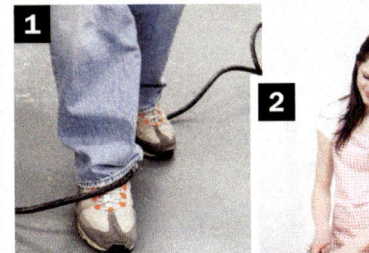

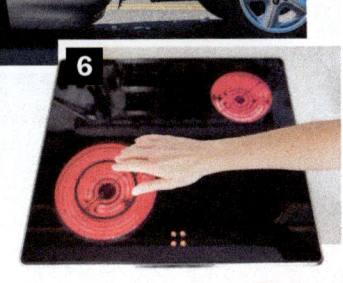

bang	burn	cut	hurt	sprain
break	crash	fall off	slip	✓ trip

1. We need to move the computer cord, so I don't ___trip___ over it.
2. Be careful! Don't _____ your finger with the knife.
3. If you _____ your leg, you'll have to use crutches.
4. Watch out! You can _____ on the ice.
5. This road is dangerous. Be careful you don't _____ your car.
6. The stove is hot. Don't _____ your hand.
7. Always wear a helmet in case you _____ your bike.
8. Look out! You're going to _____ your head!
9. If you _____ your back, you might need to see a doctor.
10. Put ice on your finger if you _____ it.

2. Listen, check, and repeat.

3. Work with a partner. Where are some common places that the accidents and injuries in Exercise 1 happen?

> People often trip over things at school.

> Yes, and they trip over things at home, too.

Speaking: It happened to me!

4. YOUR TURN Work with a partner. When was the last time the accidents and injuries in Exercise 1 happened to you or someone you know?

> I tripped over my dog yesterday!

> My dad cut his finger last week.

Workbook, p. 58

Reading It's Hard Being a Teen!; Your Invitation; Beware of the Amazon!
Conversation Reacting to good and bad news
Writing An email to refuse an invitation

STAY Safe!

It's Hard Being a Teen!

Being a teenager can be difficult – *and dangerous!* The most common injuries for teens are breaking their bones, banging their heads, and getting cuts and burns. Here are some common ways these injuries happen.

Bicycle Accidents

Many teens fall off their bikes. This can cause minor or serious injuries. Many bicycle injuries have happened when teens weren't wearing helmets. If you ride a bike, always wear a helmet!

Car Crashes

Teens have had more car crashes than any other age group. One problem is texting. In the United States, over 30 percent of teens have texted while driving. This causes many accidents. Don't text and drive! And always wear a seatbelt!

Kitchen Accidents

It's easy to cut a finger with a knife. However, burns are the most common kitchen injury. People have burned themselves on the stove or with hot liquids when they weren't careful. Teens need to be careful in the kitchen!

Sports Injuries

Exercise is good for you, but it can also be dangerous. Many teens get injuries when they play sports. Injuries in winter sports, like snowboarding and skiing, are very common. In the past, most snowboarding injuries have happened to people under 30. If you play sports, you'll want to wear protective equipment.

So, be careful and be safe . . . on the street, at home, and on the soccer field!

DID YOU KNOW . . . ?
The younger you are, the faster you heal! Children and teens recover from injuries more quickly than adults.

NOTICE IT
Many accident and injury words are both nouns and verbs.
I **burned** my finger.
It was a bad **burn**.

Reading: Common teen injuries and accidents

1. Work with a partner. Look at the title, subtitles, and photos. What do you think the article is about?

2. Read and listen to the article. Where do teens often get hurt?

3. Read the article again. Check the common injuries and accidents for teens.

Common injuries	Common accidents
☐ spraining their hands	☐ crashing a car
☐ head injuries	☐ falling off a bike
☐ cuts	☐ falling down the stairs
☐ hurting their backs	☐ getting hurt playing a sport
☐ broken bones	☐ burning their hands on a stove
☐ burns	☐ tripping over something

4. **YOUR TURN** Work with a partner. Can you think of other common injuries and accidents?

> Many people bang their heads.

Grammar: Present perfect statements with regular and irregular verbs

5. Complete the chart.

Use the present perfect to talk about experiences that happened at an indefinite time in the past. Use has/have + the past participle to form the present perfect.

	Affirmative statements	**Negative statements**
Regular verbs	Liv **has slipped** on the ice many times. Most snowboard injuries _____ **happened** to people under 30.	Kyle _____ **burned** his hand in years. Eva**'s never burned** her hand. They **haven't crashed** a car before. I**'ve** _____ **crashed** a car.
Irregular verbs	Martin _____ **broken** his arm twice. Teens **have had** more crashes than any other age group.	Julia **hasn't cut** her finger before. Teens _____ **worn** helmets. We**'ve never seen** an accident.
Contractions	has = 's _____ = 've	

> Check your answers: Grammar reference, p. 114

6. Complete the sentences with the present perfect. The verbs in blue are irregular. Check the correct forms of these verbs on p. 121.

1. I ___'ve broken___ (broke) my arm before.
2. My parents _____ (travel) to many countries.
3. I _____ (sing) in a band for five years.
4. I _____ (slip) and _____ (fall) on the ice before.
5. My best friend _____ (write) a blog since July.
6. My cousins _____ (live) in Mexico since 2012.
7. My brother _____ (trip) over our cat many times.
8. I _____ (take) a safety class before.

7. Work with a partner. Are the sentences in Exercise 6 true for you? If not, make them negative.

> I've broken my arm before.

> Really? I've never broken my arm.

Speaking: True or false?

8. **YOUR TURN** Work with a partner. Say two true and two false things you have and haven't done before. Your partner guesses if they are true or false. Take turns.

> I've eaten snake.

> I think that's false.

> No, it's true!

9. Join another pair. Tell the pair what your partner has and hasn't done.

> Dan has eaten snake. He hasn't flown in a plane. He's never . . .

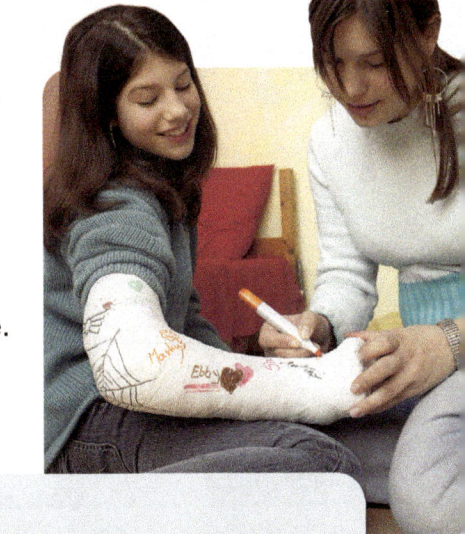

Spell it RIGHT!

Past participles For regular verbs:
+ **-ed**: bang → bang**ed**
+ **-d**: live → liv**ed**
-y → **-i** + **-ed**: study → stud**ied**
double consonant + **-ed**: trip → trip**ped**
For irregular verbs: See p. 121.

Get it RIGHT!

Do not put **never** before the verb. It goes between **has/have** and the past participle in the present perfect.
You **have never broken** your arm.
NOT: ~~You **never have broken** your arm.~~

BE CURIOUS Find out about *E. coli*. What foods can you get *E. coli* from? (Workbook, p. 88)

Discovery EDUCATION

9.1 DANGER IN OUR FOOD

Actions and ACCIDENTS

Listening: I'm accident-prone.

1. Do you and your friends do any dangerous sports or activities? What are they?

2. Listen to Angie and Franco talk about accidents and injuries. Who gets hurt easily?
   a. Franco
   b. Angie
   c. both Franco and Angie

3. Listen again. Are the sentences true (*T*) or false (*F*)?
   1. Angie has broken her arm in the past. ____
   2. She has fallen off her bike. ____
   3. She doesn't wear a helmet when she rides her bike. ____
   4. She fell off a swing when she was a baby. ____
   5. She slipped in the kitchen once. ____
   6. Franco has broken his arm. ____

Vocabulary: Parts of the body

4. Match the words (a–i) with the correct parts of the body. Then listen and repeat.

   a. an ankle
   b. an elbow
   c. a foot
   d. a knee
   ✓ e. a neck
   f. a shoulder
   g. a stomach
   h. toes
   i. a wrist

   1. e
   2. ☐
   3. ☐
   4. ☐
   5. ☐
   6. ☐
   7. ☐
   8. ☐
   9. ☐

5. What other parts of the body do you know? Make a list.

   eyes, a head, fingers ...

6. **YOUR TURN** Work with a partner. Tell your partner what parts of the body you've injured. Use these verbs and your own ideas.

   | break | burn | cut | hurt | sprain |

   I've broken my wrist, and I've sprained my knee. I've also burned my fingers.

   NOTICE IT
   The plural of *foot* is *feet*.

88 | Unit 9

Grammar: Present perfect questions; present perfect vs. simple past

7. Complete the chart.

Use the present perfect to ask questions about experiences that happened at an indefinite time in the past. Ever is often used in Yes/No questions.

Yes/No questions	Wh- questions
Have you **ever broken** an arm? Yes, I _____. / No, I **haven't**.	What bones _____ you **broken**? My wrist, my arm, and my leg.
_____ she **ever fallen** off her bike? Yes, she **has**. / No, she _____.	Why **has** she **had** accidents? Because she's clumsy.

Remember: Use the simple past, not the present perfect, for experiences that happened at a definite time in the past.

Have you ever fallen off your bike?	Yes, I have. I **fell** off my bike yesterday.
What happened the second time?	I **slipped** and **fell**. I **broke** my wrist.

> Check your answers: Grammar reference, p. 114

8. Write questions with the present perfect. The verbs in blue are irregular. Check the correct forms of these verbs on p. 121.

1. you / ever / lose / your keys — *Have you ever lost your keys?*
2. your parents / ever / live / in another city _____
3. your / best friend / fall off / a bike _____
4. you / ever / slip on something _____
5. what bones / you / break _____
6. where / your teacher / travel _____

9. Work with a partner. Ask and answer the questions in Exercise 8.

> Have you ever lost your keys?

> Yes, I have.

10. Circle the correct words.

1. **It's stopped** / It stopped raining. Let's ride our bikes.
2. **I've never tried** / **I didn't try** snowboarding. I'd love to do that.
3. My mom **has read** / **read** a good book last week.
4. When **have you hurt** / **did you hurt** your foot?
5. My brother **has banged** / **banged** his knee a lot. He's accident-prone.

Say it RIGHT!
In *Wh-* questions, **have** often sounds like /əv/. Listen to the questions.

Where **have** you been?
What **have** you seen?

Pay attention to the way you pronounce **have** in Exercise 11.

Speaking: Have you ever . . . ?

11. YOUR TURN Work with a partner. Ask and answer questions in the present perfect. Use the phrases from the box or your own ideas. Add additional information in the simple past.

| climb a mountain | have a pet | try an adventure sport | try Mexican food |

> Have you ever tried an adventure sport?

> What sport have you tried?

> Yes, I have.

> I went globe riding two years ago. I loved it!

> Workbook, pp. 60–61

REAL TALK 9.2 HAVE YOU EVER HAD AN ACCIDENT?

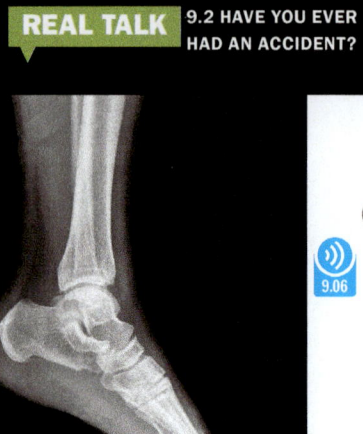

A Dangerous TRIP?

Conversation: Good news, bad news

1. **REAL TALK** Watch or listen to the teenagers. Check the accidents and injuries they've had.

   ☐ broken an arm   ☐ cut a foot   ☐ fell out of a tree   ☐ tripped over a skateboard
   ☐ broken a leg   ☐ cut a hand   ☐ sprained a wrist
   ☐ burned a hand   ☐ fell off a bike   ☐ sprained an ankle

2. **YOUR TURN** Have *you* ever had an accident? Tell your partner.

3. Holly is telling Theo some news. Listen and complete the conversation.

USEFUL LANGUAGE: Reacting to good and bad news

I'm sorry to hear that.   That's too bad.   That sounds like fun.   That's cool!

Theo: Hi, Holly. How's it going?
Holly: Well . . . I have good news, and I have bad news.
Theo: What happened?
Holly: I'll start with the bad news. I **fell on a ski trip** and **sprained my ankle**.
Theo: ¹_____ So, what's the good news?
Holly: I met a new friend at the hospital. She's really nice.
Theo: ²_____ But, what happened to her?
Holly: She **tripped over some shoes** and **broke her arm**.
Theo: Oh, no! ³_____
Holly: I know. But we've texted each other a lot, and we're **going to the beach** this weekend.
Theo: ⁴_____

4. Practice the conversation with a partner.

5. **YOUR TURN** Repeat the conversation in Exercise 3, but change the words in purple. Use the information in the chart for one conversation and your own ideas for another.

		My ideas
First accident	fell off my skateboard at a competition	
First injury	cut my leg	
Second accident	slipped on the stairs	
Second injury	hurt her knee	
Activity	seeing a movie	

To: TedR12@middleschool.cup.org
From: garytruss@net.cup.org
Subject: Your invitation

Hi Ted,

Thanks for inviting me to the amusement park on Saturday. I'm sorry, but I can't go with you. My family is going on a trip with real danger. We're going to swim with sharks this weekend! Have you ever done that?

I've taken diving classes for two years. I've been on a lot of dives, but I've never seen sharks. Actually, it will be safe. We're going with a diving instructor, and we'll be in cages. But it's still scary! Look at the photo I sent from the diving website.

Again, I'm really sorry. Have a great time! Maybe we can go to the amusement park together in July.

Your friend,

Gary

Reading to write: An email to refuse an invitation

6. Look at the photo. What do you think Gary is going to do? Read his email to check.

⊙ Focus on CONTENT
When you refuse an invitation:
- thank the person for the invitation
- apologize at the beginning of the note
- explain why you can't accept the invitation
- apologize again at the end of the note
- suggest another time to do something

7. Read Gary's email again. Why can't he go to the amusement park? When does he suggest going to the amusement park with Ted?

⊙ Focus on LANGUAGE
You can use these phrases to refuse an invitation.
To thank someone:
Thanks for inviting me to . . .
Thank you for the invitation to . . .
To apologize and refuse:
I'm sorry, but I . . .   *I'd love to come, but . . .*
Sorry, but I'm busy . . . *I'm really sorry.*
To suggest another time:
Could we go . . . ?   *Maybe we can . . .*
How about another time?

8. Which phrases in the Focus on Language box does Gary use in his email?

9. Circle the correct words.

¹**Thanks / Sorry** for the invitation to your pool party. ²**Maybe we can / I'd love to** come, but I broke my leg last week. I can't get my cast wet, and the doctor said I have to stay off my leg for several weeks.
I'm really ³**busy / sorry**. I hope you have a great birthday and party. ⁴**How about / Thanks for** another time? ⁵**Sorry / Maybe** I can come over and swim in a few months.

✏ Writing: Your email to refuse an invitation

◻ PLAN
Your friend invited you to an event, and you can't go. Write notes about it with your own ideas.

The event	
Why you can't go	
Another time you could go	

◻ WRITE
Write your email. Use your notes to help you. Write at least 80 words.

◻ CHECK
Check your writing. Can you answer "yes" to these questions?

- Is information for each category from the Focus on Content box in your email?

- Do you use expressions from the Focus on Language box correctly?

Workbook, pp. 62–63

BEWARE OF THE AMAZON!

Millions of people have visited the Amazon rain forest, and more will visit in the future. They have seen tiny insects, beautiful birds, and playful monkeys. But some Amazon animals are very dangerous!

HOME | Virtual Tour | About Us | Contact Us | FAQs

BRAZILIAN WANDERING SPIDERS aren't very big, but they are very dangerous! Some say they are the most poisonous spiders in the world! Don't let this scary creature bite your hands or feet.

As you can tell from the name, **POISON DART FROGS** are also poisonous. They don't bite, but these cute and colorful frogs have poisonous skin. Their bright colors tell other animals, "Watch out! I'm poisonous. Don't eat me!" The golden poison dart frog is only about five centimeters long, but its skin has enough poison to kill 10 people!

ANACONDAS aren't small. They're very big snakes, and they never stop growing. People have seen anacondas up to 6.5 meters long. They aren't poisonous, but they are definitely dangerous. They squeeze animals and then eat them whole! People have found birds, pigs, and jaguars in their stomachs!

JAGUARS are big and beautiful cats, and they can kill. They are the third biggest cat in the world, after lions and tigers. They eat more than 80 different kinds of animals. They've even eaten anacondas!

So, who would win a fight between an anaconda and a jaguar? Either animal could win. But it's the tiny **MOSQUITO** that is the most dangerous animal in the rain forest. You can become very sick or even die from a mosquito bite.

Watch out for these dangerous Amazon animals - big and small!

Culture: Dangerous rain forest animals

1. Look at the title and the photos. How do you think these animals are similar? How are they different?

2. Read and listen to the article. Which Amazon animals are small? Which ones are big?
   9.08

3. Read the article again. Answer the questions.
   1. Which animals are poisonous? _____
   2. Why is the poison dart frog's skin colorful? _____
   3. What are some animals that anacondas have eaten? _____
   4. Which cats are bigger than jaguars? _____
   5. Which animal is the most dangerous? _____

4. **YOUR TURN** Work with a partner. What are some dangerous animals in your country? What do you know about them? Have you or has someone you know ever had an experience with a dangerous animal?

DID YOU KNOW...?
Some people in the Amazon use the poison from the poison dart frog's skin in blow darts. They use the darts to hunt and kill other animals.

BE CURIOUS — Find out about some animals in Australia. Which ones are dangerous? (Workbook, p. 89)

Discovery EDUCATION
9.3 A DEADLY JOB

UNIT 9 REVIEW

Vocabulary

1. **Match the warnings with the situations.**

   1. The floor is wet. ___
   2. That box is heavy. ___
   3. The pan is hot. ___
   4. This knife is very sharp. ___
   5. That trail has a lot of rocks on it. ___
   6. There's a book on the floor. ___
   7. The ceiling is low. ___
   8. The road is dangerous. ___

   a. Don't fall off your bike.
   b. Don't bang your head.
   c. Don't hurt your back.
   d. Don't crash your car.
   e. Don't slip!
   f. Don't cut your finger.
   g. Don't trip!
   h. Don't burn your hand.

2. **Write the name for each part of the body.**

   1. _____
   2. _____
   3. _____
   4. _____
   5. _____
   6. _____
   7. _____
   8. _____
   9. _____

Grammar

3. **Write negative sentences two ways.**

   1. I / not slip / on ice   *I haven't slipped on ice.*
      I've never slipped on ice.
   2. Jake / not burn / his arm
      _____
      _____
   3. we / not fall / off our bikes
      _____
      _____
   4. my parents / not crash / their car
      _____
      _____
   5. you / not hurt / your back
      _____
      _____

4. **Complete the conversation with the present perfect or the simple past.**

   Jim: ¹_____ you ever _____ (be) scuba diving?
   Lia: No, I ²_____. Have you?
   Jim: Yes, I ³_____. I ⁴_____ (go) scuba diving last week.
   Lia: Cool! ⁵_____ you _____ (like) it?
   Jim: Yes. I ⁶_____ (love) it!
   Lia: I ⁷_____ never _____ (do) any adventure sports.
   Jim: Do you want to?
   Lia: Not really.

Useful language

5. **Circle the correct words.**

   1. **A:** I fell off a ladder last week.
      B: That sounds like fun. / That's too bad. Are you OK?
   2. **A:** I'm going to the Amazon rain forest next month.
      B: That's cool! / That's too bad!
   3. **A:** My mother slipped and broke her arm.
      B: I'm sorry to hear that. / That's cool.
   4. **A:** My family is going to go hiking this weekend.
      B: I'm sorry to hear that. / That sounds like fun.

PROGRESS CHECK: Now I can . . .

☐ talk about accidents and injuries.
☐ talk about things I have and haven't done.
☐ ask, answer, and give details about things I've done.
☐ react to good and bad news.
☐ write an email to refuse an invitation.
☐ talk about dangerous animals.

10 Have Fun!

Discovery EDUCATION

BE CURIOUS

- A New York City Food Tour
- How do you celebrate your birthday?
- Punkin Chunkin!
- An Ancient Answer

1. Where are the teens?
2. What are they doing? Are they having fun?
3. What do you do for fun?

UNIT CONTENTS
Vocabulary Free-time activities; adjectives of feeling
Grammar Indefinite pronouns; *too* and *enough*
Listening I'll never forget . . .

Vocabulary: Free-time activities

1. Label the pictures with the correct phrases.

celebrate your birthday   have a party   play video games   spend time with your family
go to a dance   listen to music   read books   take photos
✓ hang out with friends   play an instrument

1. _____
2. _____ 
3. _____ 
4. _____ 
5. _____ 
6. _____ 
7. _hang out with friends_ and _____ 
8. _____ and _____ 

2. Listen, check, and repeat.

3. Work with a partner. Where do you usually do the activities in Exercise 1? Are there any activities you don't do?

> I listen to music alone in my room. I don't go to dances.

Speaking: Top 5

4. YOUR TURN Work with a group. What are your top five favorite activities from Exercise 1? Which one is the most popular with the group?

> My top five favorite activities are taking photos, celebrating . . .

Workbook, p. 64

Reading Jodi's Blog; Your Invitation; April Fool's!
Conversation Making and responding to suggestions
Writing An invitation

Weekend FUN

JODI'S BLOG

I want to go somewhere fun this weekend. I'll go anywhere in the city or close by. Does anyone have a good idea? Please post a picture if you have one!

VERONICA RAMIREZ
Go to the outdoor community swimming pool. It's a great place to spend time with your family or hang out with friends. There's something for everyone there! You can swim, sit in the sun and read a book, or go to the café for a snack. I always have a good time there!

MIKE BENSON
Why don't you listen to music on Saturday – live music! I'm in a band with my friends, and we're playing at Roks Café at 9:00 p.m. We all play different instruments. I play the drums, my friend Joe plays the piano, and Cassandra plays the guitar and sings. Come and listen to us and bring someone with you. Hey – if anyone knows about future gigs, we'll play anywhere! 🙂

JASON PETERS
You could go power kiting in the park. It's a cool, new sport, and it's a lot of fun! I went last weekend, and I've never done anything like it before. It's a combination of skateboarding and kite flying. It looks hard, but it's actually pretty easy. The guide helps you with everything and even takes your photo while you're in the air!

DID YOU KNOW...?
The world's largest outdoor swimming pool is in Chile. It's more than 1 km long. That's the size of 20 Olympic swimming pools.

Reading: Weekend plans

1. Work with a partner. Look at the photos. Which activity looks like the most fun?

2. Read and listen to the article. What does each person suggest for Jodi?

3. Read the article again. Who does or did these things? Check (✓) the correct names. Sometimes more than one answer is possible.

	Veronica	Mike	Jason
does an outdoor activity			
spends time with his/her family			
plays an instrument			
does a sport			
does an activity with friends			

4. **YOUR TURN** Work with a partner. What fun things can you do on the weekend in your city or in other areas?

> You can go to an amusement park and . . .

Grammar: Indefinite pronouns

5. Complete the chart.

Use indefinite pronouns for people, places, and things that are not specific.

	People	Places	Things
some-	_____	somewhere	something
every-	everyone	everywhere	_____
no-	no one	nowhere	nothing
any-	anyone	_____	anything
	Bring **someone** with you.	I want to go **somewhere** fun.	He helps you with **everything**.
	No one has an idea.	We'll play **anywhere**.	I've never done **anything** like it.

> Check your answers: Grammar reference, p. 115

6. Replace the underlined words with an indefinite pronoun.

1. I think there's <s>a person</s> at the door. *someone*
2. Where's Jack? He's in a room in the house, I think.
3. I've looked for my bag in all the places in my room. I can't find it in any place.
4. There's no food in the fridge.
5. Ouch! I have a small object in my shoe!
6. There's not one place to listen to music in this town.

7. Circle the correct words.

Edinburgh, Scotland, is an amazing city. ¹**(Anyone)** / **Anything** could have fun there. It's the world capital of festivals. There's a festival for ²**everything** / **everywhere**, and there's always ³**something** / **somewhere** to do. In the summer, it has the biggest arts festival in the world. There are thousands of events ⁴**everything** / **everywhere** in the city. Many of the outdoor shows are free. In the winter, the Scottish New Year party is a three-day festival that ⁵**everything** / **everyone** goes to. ⁶**Nowhere** / **No one** wants to miss it! If you don't have ⁷**nothing** / **anything** better to do this summer, go to Edinburgh!

Speaking: Fun in my town

8. YOUR TURN Work with a partner. Think of the following things for your town.

- an area where there's nothing to do
- a place everyone likes to go
- a place no one likes to go
- a place that sells everything for computers
- a place you can buy anything you need
- someone famous from your town
- something to do on the weekend
- somewhere to play sports

> Clinton Park is somewhere you can play sports.
>
> So is City Stadium.

Get it RIGHT!

Use indefinite pronouns with **any-**, not **no-**, in negative sentences.
I **didn't show anyone** the photo.
NOT: I <s>didn't show no one</s> the photo.
I **didn't go anywhere** on vacation.
NOT: I <s>didn't go nowhere</s> on vacation.
I **didn't do anything** with my friends.
NOT: I <s>didn't do nothing</s> <s>with my friends</s>.

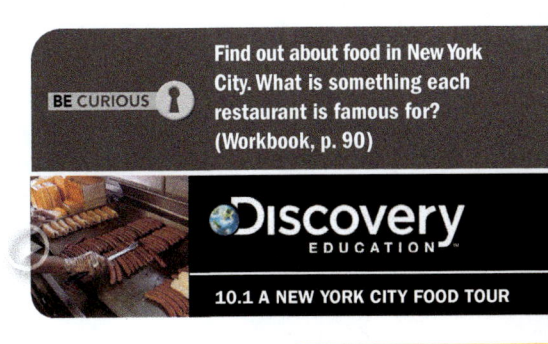

BE CURIOUS — Find out about food in New York City. What is something each restaurant is famous for? (Workbook, p. 90)

Discovery EDUCATION
10.1 A NEW YORK CITY FOOD TOUR

Workbook, p. 65

Exciting TRIPS

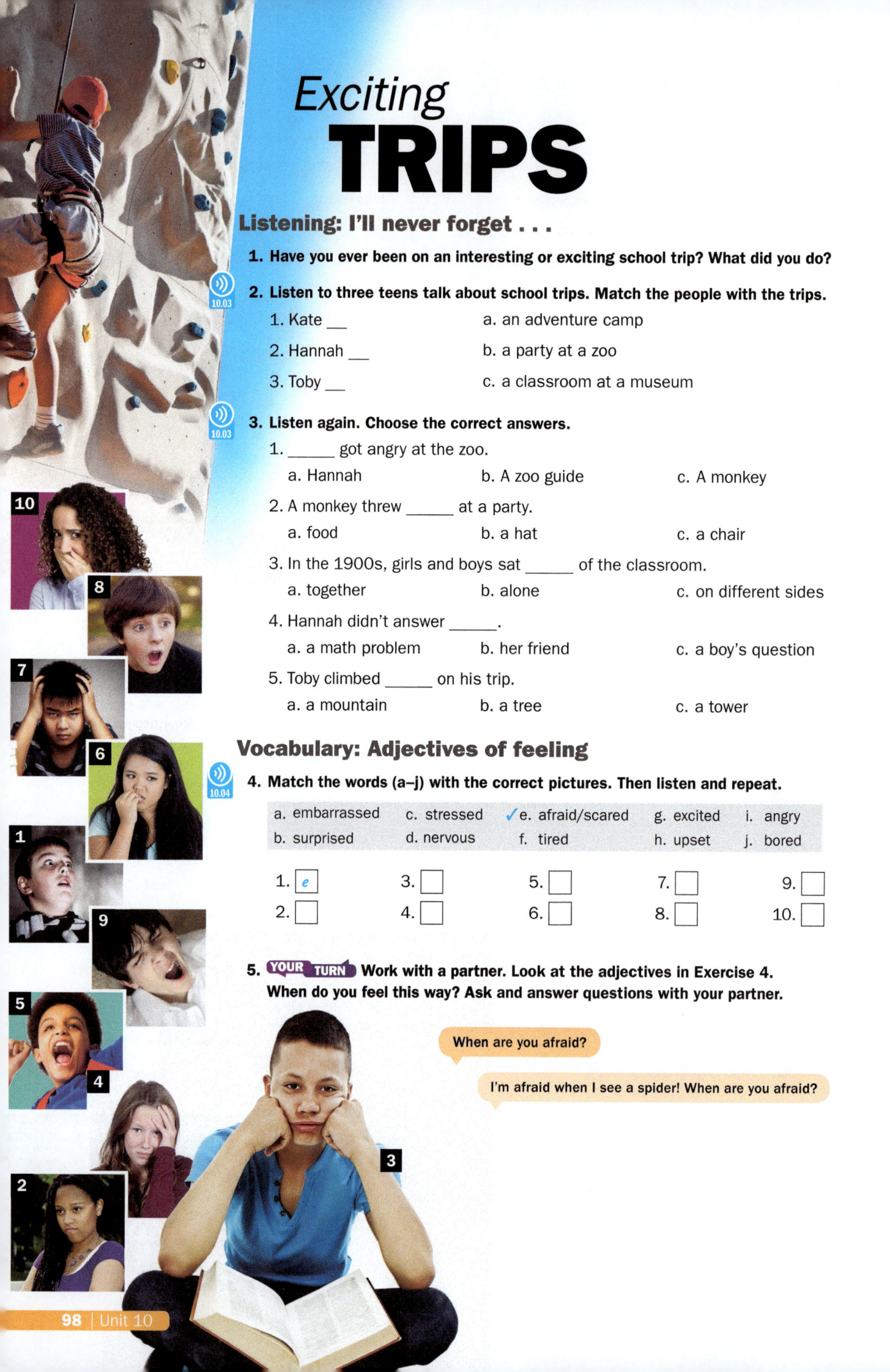

Listening: I'll never forget . . .

1. Have you ever been on an interesting or exciting school trip? What did you do?

2. Listen to three teens talk about school trips. Match the people with the trips.

   1. Kate ___
   2. Hannah ___
   3. Toby ___

   a. an adventure camp
   b. a party at a zoo
   c. a classroom at a museum

3. Listen again. Choose the correct answers.
   1. _____ got angry at the zoo.
      a. Hannah   b. A zoo guide   c. A monkey
   2. A monkey threw _____ at a party.
      a. food   b. a hat   c. a chair
   3. In the 1900s, girls and boys sat _____ of the classroom.
      a. together   b. alone   c. on different sides
   4. Hannah didn't answer _____.
      a. a math problem b. her friend   c. a boy's question
   5. Toby climbed _____ on his trip.
      a. a mountain   b. a tree   c. a tower

Vocabulary: Adjectives of feeling

4. Match the words (a–j) with the correct pictures. Then listen and repeat.

a. embarrassed	c. stressed	✓ e. afraid/scared	g. excited	i. angry
b. surprised	d. nervous	f. tired	h. upset	j. bored

   1. *e*   3. ☐   5. ☐   7. ☐   9. ☐
   2. ☐   4. ☐   6. ☐   8. ☐   10. ☐

5. **YOUR TURN** Work with a partner. Look at the adjectives in Exercise 4. When do you feel this way? Ask and answer questions with your partner.

   > When are you afraid?

   > I'm afraid when I see a spider! When are you afraid?

Grammar: too and enough

6. Complete the chart.

> Use *too + adjective + infinitive* to show something is more than what we want or need.
> Use *adjective + enough + infinitive* to show something is what we want or need. *Not enough* shows something is less than we want or need.

too	enough
I was **too scared** _____ answer.	I was **strong** _____ **to do** it.
They were _____ **nervous to try** something.	The monkey wasn't **big enough** _____ **reach** the food.

▶ Check your answers: Grammar reference, p. 115

7. Complete the sentences with *too + adjective + infinitive*.

| angry | cold | ✓ scared | stressed | tired |

1. Yolanda is <u>too scared to watch</u> (watch) the horror movie!
2. I don't want to go in the water because it's _____ (swim).
3. We rode bikes all morning. We're _____ (go) on a hike.
4. You're _____ (talk) to me now. Call me when you're calmer.
5. Jeff is _____ (have) fun; he needs to relax.

8. Complete the sentences with *(not) enough + the adjectives and verbs*.

1. We can't have a picnic because it's <u>not warm enough to eat</u> (warm / eat) outside.
2. Lilly is _____ (young / get) into the museum for free. She has to buy a ticket.
3. I was _____ (tired / fall) asleep on the train. I missed my stop!
4. My sister is _____ (old / drive). Maybe she can take us to the mall.
5. I'm _____ (tall / reach) my suitcase. Can you get it for me, please?

9. Circle the correct words.

1. Don't go in the ocean. It's **not dangerous enough / (too dangerous)** to swim.
2. I'm going to bed. I'm **tired enough / too tired** to watch TV.
3. Victor was sick yesterday, but he's **well enough / too well** to go to school today.
4. You can't move that box. You're **not strong enough / too strong**.
5. Jan is **not embarrassed enough / too embarrassed** to sing in the musical.

Speaking: Are you old enough?

10. YOUR TURN Work with a partner. Use these phrases to describe yourself or someone you know.

(not) hungry enough to . . .
(not) old enough to . . .
(not) strong enough to . . .

too embarrassed to . . .
too scared to . . .
too tired to . . .

> I'm not old enough to drive.

> My little brother's too scared to go snowboarding.

Say it RIGHT!
The letters **gh** can be silent or make the /f/ sound. They make the /f/ sound in **enough**. Listen to the sentence.

/haɪ/ /ɪnʌf/

The ladder isn't **high enough** to reach the window.

Pay attention to the way you pronounce **enough** in Exercise 10.

REAL TALK 10.2 HOW DO YOU CELEBRATE YOUR BIRTHDAY?

Let's CELEBRATE!

Conversation: Birthday plans

1. **REAL TALK** Watch or listen to the teenagers. How do, did, or will they celebrate their birthdays? Number the activities in the order you hear them.

   ___ took an exam   ___ has a big party
   ___ is going to have a dance party   ___ had a pink party
   ___ prefers to celebrate at home   ___ goes on a trip

2. **YOUR TURN** How do *you* celebrate *your* birthday? Tell your partner.

3. Molly and Paul are talking about birthday plans. Listen and complete the conversation.

> **USEFUL LANGUAGE: Making and responding to suggestions**
> I'd rather   That's a great idea!   How about   Why don't we

Molly: What should we do for your birthday?
Paul: I don't know. I want to have a party and do something fun.
Molly: OK. Who are you inviting?
Paul: My **friends and a few people in my family**.
Molly: ¹_____ go to the beach? We can **have a picnic**.
Paul: ²_____ do something more exciting.
Molly: OK. Let's see . . . we could **go to the water park**.
Paul: Hmm . . . I've done that several times before. I want to do something really different.
Molly: Hey, here's an idea . . . ³_____ **paintball**?
Paul: ⁴_____ Everyone will like that.
Molly: Great. I'll email the invitations.
Paul: Cool. Thanks.

4. Practice the conversation with a partner.

5. **YOUR TURN** Repeat the conversation in Exercise 3, but change the words in purple. Use the information in the chart for one conversation and your own ideas for another.

		My ideas
Who you're inviting	my cousins and my best friend	
First suggestion	go to the mountains	
Activity for first suggestion	go horseback riding	
Second suggestion	ice-skating	
Third suggestion	miniature golf	

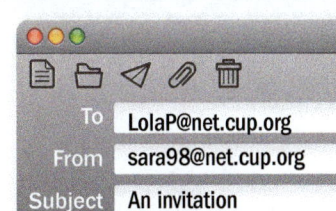

To: LolaP@net.cup.org
From: sara98@net.cup.org
Subject: An invitation

Hi Lola,

How were your exams? I'm glad to be done with them. I did well enough to pass, but the math and history ones were really hard.

Anyway, I'm having a party to celebrate the end of the school year, and I'd like you to come. It's on June 23 at Mario's Restaurant. It's the one behind the movie theater. We're meeting there at 7:00 p.m. We'll have pizza and listen to live music after dinner.

I invited 20 people. I hope everyone can come! The room is big enough for 25 people, so you can invite a friend.

On Thursday, I have to tell the restaurant how many people are coming. Please let me know by then if you can come.

Your friend,
Sara

Reading to write: An invitation

6. Look at the photo. What do you think Sara is inviting Lola to do? Read Sara's email to check.

Focus on CONTENT
When you write an invitation:
- give the event
- give the reason for the event
- give the details of the event
- ask for a response

7. Read Sara's email again. What is the event? Why is she having it? Where and when is it? What activities will there be?

Focus on LANGUAGE
You can use *referencing words* when you don't want to repeat a noun.
Pronouns:
I bought **a guitar**, but I haven't learned to play **it**.
One/Ones:
You take great **photos**. I like the black and white **ones**.
Then:
Joe's birthday is on **Friday**. I need to buy him a gift. I hope I have time to buy something before **then**.
There:
We're meeting at the **ice-skating rink**. See you **there**!

8. What nouns do the underlined referencing words in Sara's email refer to?

9. Circle the correct words.
1. I need a new book to read. Can you suggest any good **them / ones**?
2. I like to hang out with friends at The Get Away Café. Have you been **it / there**?
3. I have six cousins. I love to spend time with **them / then**.
4. Here's an invitation to my party. I'm sorry I didn't give **it / then** to you sooner.

Writing: Your invitation

PLAN
You are going to invite your friend to a fun event. Think of an event and write notes about it.

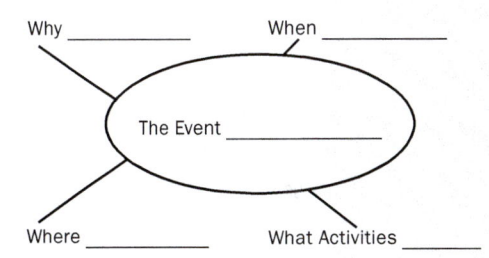

Why _____   When _____

The Event _____

Where _____   What Activities _____

WRITE
Write your invitation. Use your notes to help you. Write at least 80 words.

CHECK
Check your writing. Can you answer "yes" to these questions?

- Is information for each category from the Focus on Content box in your invitation?
- Do you use referencing words correctly?

Workbook, pp. 68–69

APRIL FOOL'S!

Be careful! Today is April 1. Don't listen to your friends when they say school's closed for a week. Don't run to the window if your brother tells you it's snowing. And don't believe everything you see on TV and the Internet. *It's April Fool's Day, and you don't want to be a fool!*

April Fool's Day probably began in the 1500s in France when New Year's Day moved from April 1 to January 1. Of course, there wasn't any TV or Internet then, so some people didn't know about this change. People called anyone who still celebrated New Year's Day on April 1 a fool.

Playing jokes on April 1 became popular, and in the 1700s, this tradition spread to England, Scotland, and eventually the United States. Today, people celebrate April Fool's Day in many countries around the world. News shows and Internet sites enjoy the fun, too!

A British TV station has made many April Fool's jokes. In 1957, it showed a program about spaghetti growing on trees. A lot of people thought it was true and called the station to ask where they could buy the trees. In 1980, reporters said that Big Ben, the famous clock in London, had a new digital face. Everyone was angry until the reporters told them it was an April Fool's joke!

An Internet company is also famous for its April Fool's Day jokes. In 2014, it advertised a keyboard for cats to use so they could type on computers. That same year, the company said it was making a "magic hand" – a robot that types on your cell phone for you. Both inventions were jokes!

Have you ever been foolish enough to believe an April Fool's Day joke?

Culture: April Fool's Day

1. **Look at the photos. What do you see? Which ones do you think are pictures of real things?**

2. **Read and listen to the article. Which is NOT an April Fool's Day joke in the article?**
   a. A clock gets a digital face.
   b. You can buy a keyboard for your cat.
   c. You can smell things on the Internet.
   d. Spaghetti grows on trees.

3. **Read the article again. Choose the correct answers to the questions.**
   1. On April Fool's Day, people _____.
      a. don't go to school
      b. play jokes on each other
      c. have a party
   2. Before the 1500s, New Year's Day was on _____.
      a. April 1
      b. January 1
      c. two different days
   3. _____ believed the joke about spaghetti growing on trees.
      a. Everyone
      b. No one
      c. Some people

4. **YOUR TURN** Work with a partner. Think of two April Fool's Day jokes to tell people.

   > We can tell people that monkeys can talk.

   > Yes. And we can make a video . . .

DID YOU KNOW...?
One of the first April Fool's Day jokes was to send people to parties that weren't really happening.

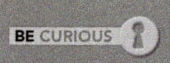

BE CURIOUS Find out about a pumpkin-throwing competition. What are the rules? (Workbook, p. 91)

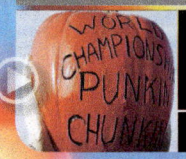

Discovery EDUCATION
10.3 PUNKIN CHUNKIN!

102 | Unit 10

UNIT 10 REVIEW

Vocabulary

1. Label the pictures with the correct phrases.

celebrate a birthday	play video games
go to a dance	read books
listen to music	take photos

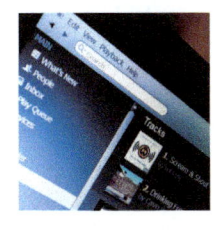

1. _____
2. _____
3. _____
4. _____
5. _____
6. _____

2. Complete the sentences.

| angry | nervous | tired |
| embarrassed | scared | |

1. Susan's really _____. She went to bed late last night.
2. Tim is _____ of spiders, especially the big ones!
3. Nina is _____ about playing in her first concert tonight.
4. Julie's teacher was very _____ because Julie was late for class again.
5. Brett was _____ because he forgot his grandma's birthday.

Grammar

3. Complete the sentences with the words in parentheses and -one, -thing, or -where.

1. I like _____ (every) in this store. I want to buy it all!
2. We didn't see Ken _____ (any).
3. _____ (every) at the park had fun.
4. There is _____ (no) to eat here.

4. Complete the sentences with enough or too + adjectives and verbs.

1. I'm _____ (scared / go) into the ocean.
2. We're not _____ (strong / lift) that box.
3. He felt _____ (sick / go) to school this morning.
4. My brother runs _____ (fast / win) the race.

Useful language

5. Complete the conversation.

| How about | I'd rather | That's a great idea | Why don't we |

Shel: What do you want to do today?
Andy: ¹_____ horseback riding?
Shel: I don't think so. ²_____ do something inside.
Andy: OK. ³_____ go to the mall?
Shel: ⁴_____! We can shop and then eat lunch.

PROGRESS CHECK: Now I can . . .

- ☐ talk about free-time activities.
- ☐ talk about weekend plans.
- ☐ describe feelings and situations with *too* and *enough*.
- ☐ make and respond to suggestions.
- ☐ write an invitation.
- ☐ talk about April Fool's Day and jokes.

▶ REVIEW UNITS 9–10, Workbook, pp. 70–71

CLIL PROJECT

10.4 An Ancient Answer, p. 120

Uncover Your Knowledge
UNITS 6–10 Review Game

TEAM 1 START

- GRAMMAR
- VOCABULARY
- USEFUL LANGUAGE

1. Tell a teammate three sentences about how to use an appliance. Use *should (not)*, *have (not)*, and *must (not)*.

2. In 30 seconds, name five appliances you can find in a kitchen.

3. Role-play a conversation with a teammate. Ask for and offer to help clean the house.

4. What technology will we have in the future? Make five predictions. Use adverbs of possibility, such as *definitely, certainly, probably, maybe,* and *perhaps*.

5. In 30 seconds, give five examples of computers and communications devices people use today.

6. Role-play a conversation with a teammate. Pretend one of you has never used a smartphone to text. Ask for and give instructions on how to send a text.

7. In one minute, name 10 life events.

8. Think of your favorite website. Tell a teammate how to find it on the Internet and use it. Use technology verbs.

9. Pretend you aren't familiar with today's technology. Ask a teammate for instructions on how to use a computer or tablet.

10. Have a conversation with a teammate. Talk about what you will be doing in five years. Use *be going to* and *will*.

11. Make three statements about your future using the first conditional. Use *will (not)*, *may (not)*, or *might (not)*.

TEAM 2
START

Role-play a conversation with a teammate. For every suggestion about something to do, offer a counter-suggestion. See how long you can keep the conversation going.

Role-play with a teammate. Act out five different feelings, and your teammate guesses the adjective.

Role-play a conversation with a teammate. Take turns telling each other about an accident or injury you had. Use expressions like *That's too bad* or *I'm sorry to hear that* to react to the bad news.

Tell a teammate six of your favorite free-time activities.

Give clues using indefinite pronouns to get your teammate to name a person, a place, or a thing (for example, *it's something many people enjoy watching: this year it will take place somewhere fun.*)

Play good news/bad news. Tell a teammate something good or bad that happened. Your teammate has to respond quickly to the news. See how many you can say in two minutes.

Point to and name nine parts of the body.

Ask a teammate four questions about his/her past. Use the question *Have you ever . . . ?* Your teammate answers.

With a teammate, make three statements about the environment and recycling. Agree and disagree with each other.

In 30 seconds, name five ways someone can get hurt. Use accident verbs.

Use the present continuous to ask a teammate about his/her future plans. Then use the simple present to ask when the events will happen.

How can you agree or disagree in a conversation? Give two examples of each.

INSTRUCTIONS:

■ Make teams and choose game pieces.

■ Put your game pieces on your team's START.

■ Flip a coin to see who goes first.

■ Read the first challenge. Can you do it correctly?

   Yes → Continue to the next challenge.

   No → Lose your turn.

The first team to do all of the challenges wins!

Units 6–10 Review | 105

This page intentionally left blank.

Comparative and superlative adjectives and adverbs, p. 57

Use comparative adjectives and adverbs to show how two things are different from each other.
Use superlative adjectives and adverbs to compare three or more things.

	Comparative	Superlative
Adjectives	dark → dark**er** big → big**ger** powerful → **more** powerful good → **better** bad → **worse** The Rio Negro is **darker than** the Rio Solimões.	dark → **the** dark**est** big → **the** big**gest** popular → **the most** popular good → **the best** bad → **the worst** The bathroom is **the darkest** room in the hotel.
Adverbs	fast → fast**er** slowly → **more** slowly far → far**ther** well → **better** badly → **worse** The Rio Solimões runs **more slowly than** the Rio Negro.	fast → **the** fast**est** slowly → **the most** slowly far → **the** far**thest** well → **the best** badly → **the worst** The water runs **the most slowly** in the summer.

1. Complete the sentences with comparative or superlative adjectives or adverbs.

1. My bedroom is *smaller than* (small) my sister's room.
2. Ramon fits _____ (well) in that chair than his father does.
3. We all eat quickly in my family, but my older brother eats _____ (quickly).
4. We stayed at _____ (bad) hotel in the city.
5. I run _____ (fast) my brother.
6. Scott is _____ (powerful) player on the team.

should (not), (not) have to, must (not), p. 59

Use should (not) for advice and recommendations. Use have to for responsibilities.
Use not have to for things that are not required. Use must for obligation. Use must not for prohibition.

Affirmative	Negative
You **should wash** dark clothes separately.	You **shouldn't wash** darker clothes with lighter ones.
She **should look** at the labels.	She **shouldn't put** it in a sunny room.
You **have to choose** the temperature first.	You **don't have to wash** it by hand.
It **has to be** cool.	It **doesn't have to be** cold.
You **must use** cold water.	You **must not (mustn't) use** hot water.
They **must follow** the directions.	They **must not (mustn't) miss** a step.

2. Complete the conversations with *should (not), (not) have to,* or *must (not)* and the verb.

stay
1. You _____ in the Hotel Flores. It's wonderful!
2. Carla _____ in a hotel on her trip. She's staying with a friend.
3. We _____ in a hotel downtown. It's really dangerous.

put
4. I _____ the dishes in the dishwasher before I go out.
5. She _____ her full name on the form. She's not allowed to use a nickname.
6. You _____ that information on the Internet. It's against the law.

will and won't for predictions, p. 67

	Wh- questions	Affirmative answers	Negative answers
	Use will and won't to predict future events.		
	What **will** my smartphone **do** in the future?	Perhaps it**'ll think** like a human.	It **won't drive** a car.
	How **will** you/I/he/she/it/they/we **change**?	You/I/He/She/It/They/We **will be** smaller.	You/I/He/She/It/They/We **won't be** bigger.
	Yes/No questions	Short answers	
	Will my smartphone **think** like a human?	Yes, it **will**.	No, it **won't**.
	Will you/I/he/she/it/they/we **change**?	Yes, you/I/he/she/it/they/we **will**.	No, you/I/he/she/it/they/we **won't**.
	Contractions	I will = I'll you will = you'll he will = he'll she will = she'll it will = it'll we will = we'll they will = they'll	

1. Complete the sentences with *will* or *won't* and the verbs in parentheses.

1. Where _____ you _____ (live) in the future?
2. Computers _____ (be) faster in five years.
3. We _____ (not buy) big phones in the future.
4. _____ Janelle _____ (study) computer science?
5. Most people _____ (not use) keyboards in a few years.

First conditional with *will (not)*, *may (not)*, and *might (not)*, p. 69

Use the first conditional to show results or possible results of future actions. Use if and the simple present in the main clause, and will (not), may (not), or might (not) and the base form of a verb in the result clause.

Statements

You**'ll see** all of the choices **if** you **zoom out**.
If I **make** games, they **won't be** boring.
If I **ask** my parents, they **might get** it for me for my birthday.
I **may not get** the Ztron 2100 **if** a new model **comes** out.

Questions

What kind of games **will** you **make if** you**'re** a designer?   Action games.
If I **beat** you, **will** you **do** my homework?   Yes, I **will**. / No, I **won't**.

2. Write sentences in the first conditional with the phrases in the box.

Main clause	Result
1. I / take / the bus / to school	I / might / be / late
2. John / buy / a computer	he / will not / get / a tablet
3. you / zoom out	you / will / see / the entire town
4. Mia and Sara / share / a computer	they / may not / finish / their homework
5. I / back up / my files	I / will not / worry

1. _____
2. _____
3. _____
4. _____
5. _____

be going to and will, p. 77

Use be going to to talk about plans in the future.
Use will to talk about predictions and unplanned decisions.

be going to	will
Wh- questions and answers	
What **are** you/we/they **going to do**? I'**m**/We'**re**/You'**re**/They'**re going to study** agriculture. He/She/It **is not going to study** history.	Where **will** you/I/he/she/it/we/they **live**? I/You/He/She/It/We/They **will live** in the outback. I/You/He/She/It/We/They **won't live** in Sydney.
Yes/No questions and answers	
Are you/we/they **going to go** to Sydney? Yes, I **am**. / Yes, we/you/they **are**. No, I'**m**/we'**re**/you'**re**/they'**re not**.	**Will** you/I/he/she/it/we/they **stay** here? Yes, you/I/he/she/it/we/they **will**. No, you/I/he/she/it/we/they **won't**.
Is he/she/it **going to study** history? Yes, he/she/it **is**. / No, he/she/it **isn't**.	

1. Write questions for the answers. Use be going to or will.

1. **A:** (when / you / study) _____

   B: I'm going to study after school.

2. **A:** (they / get married / in March) _____

   B: Yes, they will.

3. **A:** (we / drive / to the library) _____

   B: No, we aren't.

4. **A:** (where / Lea / go / to college) _____

   B: She'll go to the University of Chicago.

Present continuous and simple present for future, p. 79

As with be going to, use the present continuous to talk about future plans.
Use the simple present to talk about scheduled future events.

Present continuous	Simple present
Wh- questions and answers	
What **are** you/they/we **doing** next week? I'**m**/We'**re**/You'**re**/They'**re (not) collecting** trash.	What time **do** I/you/they/we **start**? I/We/You/They **start** at 9:00 a.m. tomorrow. I/We/You/They **don't start** at 9:00 a.m. tomorrow.
Why **is** he/she **going** there? He'**s**/She'**s taking** a year off. He'**s**/She'**s not traveling**.	When **does** he/she **start** the project? He/She **starts** next week. He/She **doesn't start** tomorrow.
Yes/No questions and answers	
Are we/you/they **helping** the turtles? Yes, we/you/they **are**. No, we'**re**/you'**re**/they'**re not**.	**Do** I/you/they/we **start** at 9:00 a.m. tomorrow? Yes, I/you/they/we **do**. No, I/you/they/we **don't**.
Is he/she **taking** a year off? Yes, he/she **is**. No, he/she **isn't**.	**Does** he/she/it **start** in five minutes? Yes, he/she/it **does**. No, he/she/it **doesn't**.

2. Circle the correct words.

1. John **is working / works** on an eco-project next summer.

2. Carla and Sammy **are making / make** jewelry from old metal cans tomorrow.

3. The store **is opening / opens** at 10:00 a.m. tomorrow.

4. **Is the class starting / Does the class start** at noon on Monday?

5. Where **are they going / do they go** tomorrow?

Present perfect statements with regular and irregular verbs, p. 87

Use the present perfect to talk about experiences that happened at an indefinite time in the past. Use has/have + the past participle to form the present perfect.

	Affirmative statements	Negative statements
Regular verbs	He/She/It **has slipped** on the ice many times. Most snowboard injuries **have happened** to people under 30. I/We/They/You **have crashed** a car.	He/She **hasn't burned** his/her hand in years. He/She **has never burned** his/her hand. I/We/They/You **haven't crashed** a car before. I/We/They/You **have never crashed** a car.
Irregular verbs	He/She/It **has broken** his/her/its arm twice. I/You/We/They **have had** more crashes than any other age group.	He/She **hasn't cut** his/her finger before. Teens **haven't worn** helmets. I/You/We/They **have never seen** an accident.
Contractions	has = 's have = 've	

1. Circle the correct words.

1. Marcy **has had / has have** three broken bones.
2. Ronaldo **has gone / has went** on many exciting vacations.
3. We **have slip / have slipped** on ice in front of our house.
4. **I've haven't seen / I've never seen** an anaconda before.
5. She **haven't burned / hasn't burned** her finger.

Present perfect questions; present perfect vs. simple past, p. 89

Use the present perfect to ask questions about experiences that happened at an indefinite time in the past. Ever is often used in Yes/No questions.

Yes/No questions	Wh- questions
Have I/you/we/they **ever broken** an arm? Yes, I/you/we/they **have**. No, I/you/we/they **haven't**.	What bones **have** I/you/we/they **broken**? My wrist, my arm, and my leg.
Has he/she **ever fallen** off his/her bike? Yes, he/she **has**. / No, he/she **hasn't**.	Why **has** he/she/it **had** accidents? Because he/she/it is clumsy.
Remember: Use the simple past, not the present perfect, for experiences that happened at a definite time in the past.	
Have you ever fallen off your bike? What happened the second time?	Yes, I have. I **fell** off my bike yesterday. I **slipped** and **fell**. I **broke** my wrist.

2. Circle the correct answers.

1. Have you ever ___ off your bike?
   a. fall   b. fell   c. fallen

2. Elsa ___ a poison dart frog at the museum yesterday.
   a. saw   b. has seen   c. has saw

3. ___ you snowboard in the mountains on your trip?
   a. Do   b. Did   c. Have

4. What bones ___ you broken?
   a. did   b. has   c. have

5. Luke ___ his cousins in months.
   a. didn't see   b. hasn't seen   c. haven't seen

Indefinite pronouns, p. 97

Use indefinite pronouns for people, places, and things that are not specific.

	People	Places	Things
some-	**someone** Bring **someone** with you.	**somewhere** I want to go **somewhere** fun.	**something** I see **something** in the water.
every-	**everyone** I invited **everyone** in my class.	**everywhere** Lilly takes her phone **everywhere**.	**everything** He helps you with **everything**.
no-	**no one** **No one** has an idea.	**nowhere** Jason is **nowhere** to be found.	**nothing** We have **nothing** ready for the party.
any-	**anyone** Does **anyone** have a good idea?	**anywhere** We'll play **anywhere**.	**anything** I've never done **anything** like it.

1. **Complete the sentences with *some-*, *every-*, *no-*, or *any-* + the word in parentheses.**

   1. I looked _____ (where) in my room for my keys.
   2. _____ (one) came to the party because Ted put the wrong date on the invitation.
   3. Kate didn't say _____ (thing) about the party, so I was really surprised.
   4. I have _____ (thing) to do on Saturday, but I can meet you on Sunday.
   5. We are _____ (where) near Jeff's house. How did we get so lost?
   6. _____ (one) is at the door, but I don't know who it is.

too and *enough*, p. 99

Use too + adjective + infinitive to show something is more than want we want or need.
Use adjective + enough + infinitive to show something is what we want or need.
Not enough shows something is less than we want or need.

too	enough
I/He/She was **too scared to answer**.	I/He/She was **strong enough to do** it. You/They/We were **old enough to know** better.
You/They/We were **too nervous to try** something.	I/He/She/It was**n't big enough to reach** the food. You/They/We were**n't tall enough to get** on the ride.

2. **Circle the correct word to complete each sentence.**

   1. Vinny is **too / enough** excited to sleep.
   2. Melanie is good **too / enough** to play on the team.
   3. It's **too / enough** hot to play outside.
   4. My parents aren't old **too / enough** to retire.
   5. Are you bored **too / enough** to leave the party?
   6. It isn't **too / enough** late to see a movie.

This page intentionally left blank.

Wonders of the WORLD

1. **Label the pictures with the correct words.**

   Cairo   stone blocks   tomb   pyramid

   1 _____   2 _____   3 _____   4 _____

2. **Watch the video. Complete the sentences with the correct numbers.**

   2   3   8   20   147

   a. There are ____ giant pyramids near Cairo.

   b. ____ million people live in Cairo.

   c. People worked for ____ years to build each pyramid.

   d. The pyramid of Khufu is ____ meters tall.

   e. There are ____ million stone blocks in this pyramid.

   7.4 THE SECRET OF THE PYRAMIDS

3. **Circle the correct answers.**

   1. They are called the pyramids of ____.
      a. Cairo
      b. Giza
      c. Khufu

   2. The builders covered the top of the tallest pyramid with ____.
      a. gold
      b. silver
      c. paint

   3. Each stone block weighs as much as ____.
      a. a small car
      b. a large car
      c. a bus

   4. The pyramids were ____.
      a. homes
      b. castles
      c. tombs

PROJECT

People started building the Seven Wonders of the World more than 4,000 years ago. The only one still standing is the Pyramid of Khufu. What are the names of the other six Wonders of the World?

Choose one of the Seven Wonders of the World and find out seven interesting facts about it. Create a poster of your Wonder and present it to your class.

Inventions from the PAST

1. Look at this picture of a step well. What do you think it does? Label the picture with the correct words:

arches   roof   stairs   walkway

1. _____
2. _____
3. _____
4. _____

Discovery EDUCATION
10.4 AN ANCIENT ANSWER

2. Watch the video. Are the sentences true (*T*) or false (*F*)?

1. In northern India, the monsoon season lasts for six months every year. ____
2. Step wells are a system for collecting water. ____
3. People built step wells to collect water when it rained. ____
4. People still build step wells today. ____
5. The animals don't get enough water. ____

3. How did people build step wells? Number the events in order 1–5.

____ a. They cut steps into the earth.
____ b. They made a hole near the tree.
____ c. They looked for a tall tree.
____ d. They covered these steps with stones.
____ e. They made the hole wider at the top.

PROJECT

Read the list below. Number the inventions and discoveries from what you think are the least important (1) to the most important (10).

____ the wheel   ____ clothes
____ rope   ____ houses
____ musical instruments ____ fire
____ the boat   ____ knives
____ paint   ____ spears

Then imagine selling one of these inventions to your classmate. How will it make his or her life better? Write three reasons your classmate should buy your invention.

Uncover 2 Combo B

Lynne M. Robertson

Workbook

CAMBRIDGE UNIVERSITY PRESS

Discovery EDUCATION

6 Home, Sweet Home

VOCABULARY Furniture and other household items

1 Put the letters in the correct order to make furniture and household words.

1. DEB _____bed_____
2. SEDK _____
3. OHREWS _____
4. LOTEIT _____
5. SEBAKOCO _____
6. REDSRES _____
7. FOAS _____
8. MARACHRI _____
9. RACIH _____
10. RORMRI _____
11. LETBA _____
12. BISTNACE _____

2 Label the pictures with the words from Exercise 1.

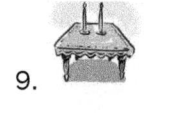

1. _____sofa_____
2. _____
3. _____
4. _____
5. _____
6. _____
7. _____
8. _____
9. _____
10. _____
11. _____
12. _____

3 Write the names of the furniture and household items from Exercise 1 in the correct columns.

Kitchen	Living room
chair	

Bathroom	Bedroom

4 Complete the sentences.

| bed | cabinets | desk | mirror | ✓sofa |

1. I sit on a _____sofa_____ when I watch TV.
2. We keep cups and glasses in _____.
3. I sleep in a _____.
4. He does his homework at a _____.
5. Who do you see in the _____?

5 Answer the questions with your own information.

1. What's in your kitchen?
   There's a table and chairs.
2. What's your favorite thing to sit on?
   _____
3. What color is your bed?
   _____
4. What's in your dresser?
   _____
5. What's your favorite piece of furniture? Why?
   _____
   _____

GRAMMAR Comparative and superlative adjectives and adverbs

1 Complete the rules and write the comparative and superlative forms of the adjectives.

1. For most comparative adjectives and adverbs with one syllable, add ____**-er**____.

   warm → ____**warmer**____

   long → _____

2. For most superlative adjectives and adverbs with one syllable, add _____.

   warm → the _____

   long → the _____

3. For most comparative adjectives and adverbs with two or more syllables, add _____.

   exciting → _____

   slowly → _____

4. For most superlatives adjectives and adverbs with two or more syllables, add _____.

   exciting → the _____

   slowly → the _____

5. Some comparative adjectives are irregular:

   good → _____

   bad → _____

6. Some superlative adjectives are irregular:

   good → the _____

   bad → the _____

7. Some comparative adverbs are irregular:

   well → _____

   badly → _____

8. Some superlative adverbs are irregular:

   well → the _____

   badly → the _____

2 Write the comparative and superlative forms of the adjectives.

Adjective	Comparative	Superlative
big	bigger	the biggest
strange		
beautiful		
exciting		

3 Write the comparative and superlative forms of the adverbs.

Adverb	Comparative	Superlative
quickly	more quickly	the most quickly
slowly		
far		
hard		

4 Complete the sentences using the comparative and superlative adjectives and adverbs.

1. My parents' living room is ____**nice**____. But my grandparents' living room is ____**nicer**____. (nice)

2. My brother's bedroom is the _____ bedroom in our house. It is _____ than our parents'. (big)

3. My sister cooks _____. But I cook _____. (well)

4. She speaks Spanish _____. But she speaks Chinese _____ Spanish. (quick)

5. In our house, the living room is _____ the dining room. But the kitchen is the _____. (popular)

6. Our bookcase is _____. But the dresser is _____. (dark)

VOCABULARY Household appliances

1 Complete the crossword puzzle with the names of household appliances.

```
        1 w
2 _ _ _ _ _ _ _ a _ _
        s
      3 h _ _ _ _ _ _
        i
    4 _ n _ _
        g
      5 m _
  6     a
    7   c   8
        h
      9 i _ _ _ _ _
        n
10 _ _ _ _ e _ _
     11 _ _ _ _ _
12 _ _ _
```

ACROSS

2.
3.
4.
5.
9.
10.
11.
12.

DOWN

1.
6.
7.
8.

2 Write the names of the household appliances.

1. This keeps your food cold. _refrigerator_
2. You use these to cook food. _____, _____, _____, _____
3. You put your dishes in this to wash them. _____
4. You clean your clothes in this. _____
5. You may need to use this on your shirt. _____
6. This is probably the first thing you hear in the morning. _____
7. You might use this after your shower. _____
8. When it's dark, you turn this on. _____
9. You clean the carpet with this. _____

3 What time of day do you use these appliances? Write the name of the appliance in the appropriate place in the word web. Add your own ideas. Some words can go in more than one circle.

| alarm clock | ✓dishwasher | hairdryer | lamp |
| microwave | refrigerator | stove | toaster |

Evening/Night
dishwasher
_____
_____

Morning
_____
_____
_____

Day
_____

Afternoon
_____

4 Write sentences about these household appliances. Use your own information.

| ✓alarm clock | dishwasher | hairdryer |
| iron | oven | vacuum cleaner |

1. I have a black __alarm clock__ in my bedroom.
2. I rarely use the _____.
3. My favorite appliance is the _____.
4. I use the _____ in the _____.
5. _____.

38 | Unit 6

GRAMMAR should (not), (not) have to, must (not)

1 Circle the correct verbs to complete the rules in the chart.

should (not), (not) have to, must (not)
1. Use **should not** / **not have to** for advice and recommendations.
2. Use **must** / **have to** for responsibilities.
3. Use **not have to** / **must not** for things that are not required.
4. Use **must** / **have to** for an obligation.
5. Use **should not** / **must not** for a prohibition.

(1. should not is circled)

2 Correct the sentences with the affirmative or negative.

1. You ~~should~~ *shouldn't* keep bananas in the refrigerator.
2. You must not set your alarm clock if you want to wake up on time.
3. You don't have to follow the directions when you wash clothes.
4. You must look at your friend's test paper.
5. You don't have to keep your room clean to earn your allowance.
6. You have to do the dishes after dinner. Your brother is going to do them.

3 Write the correct answers.

1. (recommendation) You ____should____ cook the vegetables on the stove and not in the microwave.
2. (prohibition) You _____ use the hairdryer while you're in the bathtub.
3. (responsibility) When his mother cooks, he _____ load the dishwasher after dinner.
4. (things not required) But he _____ do the dishes if he cooks dinner.
5. (obligation) Read the label. It says you _____ wash that shirt in cold water. Don't use hot water.
6. (things not required) We _____ bring a hairdryer. The hotel will have one.

4 Answer the questions. Use your own information and *should (not)*, *(not) have to*, or *must (not)* to answer the questions.

1. What advice can you give someone about how to dress today?
   You should wear a T-shirt. It's hot outside.

2. What do you recommend NOT to do in school?
   _____
   _____

3. What do you have to do every night?
   _____
   _____

4. What don't you have to do on weekends?
   _____
   _____

5. What must you NOT eat?
   _____
   _____

CONVERSATION: I have to clean the house.

1 Put the words in the correct order.

1. like / some / you / Would / help / ?
   Would you like some help?

2. Can / ask / you / a favor / I / ?
   _____

3. out / help / me / Could / you / ?
   _____

4. you / hand / a / give / I'll / .
   _____

2 Complete the conversation with the questions and statements from Exercise 1.

Tim: Are you going to the park?

Iris: Well, I want to, but you look too busy to come with me. ¹ *Would you like some help*?

Tim: Yes, I would!

Iris: OK. What can I do?

Tim: I should move the sofa to clean behind it.
² _____?

Iris: Sure. ³ _____.

Tim: Thanks. OK. And ⁴ _____ ?

Iris: Of course. What is it?

Tim: Can you put those dishes in the dishwasher?

Iris: No problem.

3 Complete the conversations with the phrases from Exercise 1. More than one answer may be possible.

1. **A:** I need a hand in the garden.
   _____
   _____?
   B: Sorry, but I'm busy right now.

2. **A:** These boxes are heavy!
   B: _____
   _____?
   A: Thanks.

3. **A:** _____
   _____?
   I need a ride to school.
   B: I can drive you.

4. **A:** I need to vacuum and put the dishes in the dishwasher.
   B: _____
   _____.
   A: Thank you!

40 | Unit 6

READING TO WRITE

1 Write the words in the correct places in the chart.

apartment	chairs	modern
armchair	desk	new
bathroom	dishwasher	old
bed	dresser	small
bedroom	house	sofa
✓big	kitchen	table
bookcase	living room	washing machine

Size, age, kind	_big_ , _____ , _____ , _____ , _____ , _____ , _____
Rooms	_____ , _____ , _____ , _____
Furniture	_____ , _____ , _____ , _____ , _____ , _____ , _____ , _____
Appliances	_____ , _____

2 Correct the comma errors in the sentences. Some sentences may not need correction.

1. There are three armchairs, and one sofa in the living room.
2. I have to turn on the dishwasher brush my hair and set the alarm clock before bed.
3. We have a dog, a cat, and a bird.
4. He washes his bike and car every weekend.
5. Please put the cups glasses and dishes in the cabinets.
6. We cleaned the bathroom bedroom living room and kitchen this morning.

3 Answer the questions about you. Use the words from Exercise 1 and your own information.

1. What kind of home do you (or your friends) live in?

   I live in an apartment. But it's in London,
   so we call it a "flat."

2. What is your home like?

   _____
   _____

3. What is in your bedroom?

   _____
   _____

4. Where in your house do you spend the most time?

   _____
   _____

5. What is your favorite piece of furniture in your home?

   _____
   _____

REVIEW UNITS 5–6

1 Match the descriptions with the correct furniture and household items. Then write the names of the items.

1. This cooks food quickly. ____
   _____

2. This helps you see when a room is dark. ____
   _____

3. This is where you wash your whole body. ____
   _____

4. You keep clothing in this. ____
   _____

5. You put bread in this. ____
   _____

6. You can sit at this to eat a meal. ____
   _____

7. You use this in the bathroom every day. ____
   _____

8. This makes washing dishes easy. ____
   _____

9. You keep things to read here. ____
   _____

10. You get into this to sleep. ____
    _____

a.
b.
c.
d.
e.
f.
g.
h.
i.
j.

2 Complete the sentences with adverbs of manner.

1. She was talking _____ on her cell phone. (loud)

2. John usually does his homework _____. (careful)

3. Ella _____ cooked dinner for her parents. (happy)

4. They were singing _____ because they were nervous. (terrible)

5. She didn't practice, so the performance went _____. (bad)

6. I studied a lot, so I did _____ on my test. (good)

3 Complete the paragraph with action verbs.

| caught | chased | fell | jumped | stole |
| caught | climbed | hid | ran | threw |

The movie started as the thief [1]_____ in the bathroom at a bank. After everyone left in the evening, he [2]_____ a lot of money and put it into a bag. He left through the back door. Then he [3]_____ up the back of the next building. From there, he [4]_____ onto the next roof. You could hear sirens. The thief's buddy was waiting for him on the ground. The thief [5]_____ the bag down to his buddy. The buddy [6]_____ it and then [7]_____ away! The police saw him and [8]_____ him. The buddy [9]_____, and the police [10]_____ him! Meanwhile, the thief was holding another bag as he watched this from the roof!

4 Circle the correct answers.

1. I can bike _____ than I can run.
   a. more quickly   b. most quickly

2. He ran _____ today than ever before.
   a. farther   b. the farthest

3. She practiced a lot, and her playing got _____.
   a. better   b. the best

4. At night, it's _____ on the farm than it is in the city.
   a. darker   b. the darkest

5. I like movies more than TV, but I like books _____.
   a. better   b. the best

5 Complete the sentences with the correct forms of the verbs. Then write *past continuous* or *simple past*.

| jump | run | sing | talk |

1. I _____ while I was in the shower. _____

2. I _____ over the log when I fell. _____

3. _____ you _____ to Jillian on the phone last night when her sister sent you a text? _____

4. _____ Alan _____ in the race yesterday? _____

6 Complete the conversation.

Can I ask you for a favor?	not have to
Could you help me out?	should not
have to	Would you like some help?
I'll give you a hand.	
must not	

Manny: Want to go to the park now?

Claire: I'd love to! But I ¹_____ do all this laundry.

Manny: ²_____

Claire: You ³_____.

Manny: I know, but I want to.

Claire: Great! I need to put all this laundry in the washing machine. ⁴_____

Manny: Sure. But wait a minute! You ⁵_____ wash light and dark colors together. You must look at the labels first!

Claire: Oh! I never do that.

Manny: ⁶_____ I'll separate the colors into light and dark.

Claire: Great. You do that. I'll get the laundry soap. Oops. ⁷_____

Manny: Sure, what is it?

Claire: Can you reach the soap?

Manny: OK. Next time you ⁸_____ put it up so high.

Claire: I didn't put it up there. I never do the laundry!

7 Visions of the Future

VOCABULARY Computers and communication

1 Find eight more computer words.

O	V	G	K	E	Y	B	O	A	R	D	F
L	Q	T	E	H	K	F	Y	P	A	O	L
T	O	U	C	H	S	C	R	E	E	N	A
L	P	T	O	U	C	H	P	A	D	E	S
Q	X	F	L	A	S	H	D	R	I	V	E
E	H	C	Y	F	T	A	B	L	E	T	D
I	M	I	T	Z	G	C	J	N	Q	Y	R
S	M	A	R	T	P	H	O	N	E	S	I
E	D	I	R	D	H	R	A	L	F	L	V
M	P	R	I	N	T	E	R	C	W	X	E
B	P	V	S	O	P	N	W	I	F	I	A
L	G	M	O	U	S	E	J	P	P	I	F

2 Complete the sentences. Use the computer words from Exercise 1.

1. You don't need a mouse for your laptop because you can use the ___touch pad___.
2. Save your work on a _____ so you can use it with another computer.
3. The _____ wasn't working, so we couldn't get on the Internet.
4. My mom prefers typing on the _____ to using the touch pad.
5. I prefer using a _____ to using a laptop.
6. I don't use my _____ very often. I email most of my assignments to my teacher.

3 Use the phrases and the computer words from Exercise 1 to write sentences.

communicate with friends	do homework
✓computing power	save information

1. _A smartphone today has more computing power than the first computers._
2. _____
3. _____
4. _____

4 Complete the sentences with your own information. Use the computer words from Exercise 1.

1. I have a ___tablet and a smartphone___.
2. I use a _____ to _____.
3. I never use a _____.
4. My parents _____.
5. My best friend _____.

44 | Unit 7

GRAMMAR will and won't for predictions

1 Rewrite the underlined phrases as contractions.

1. <u>Computers will</u> be smarter in the future.
   They'll
2. <u>This tablet will</u> get smaller in the future.

3. <u>My family will not</u> use a mouse in the future.

4. <u>You will not</u> cook your own meals.

5. <u>He will</u> use his smartphone to buy everything.

GRAMMAR Adverbs of possibility

2 Complete the chart using the adverbs of possibility.

| certainly | maybe | probably |
| ✓definitely | perhaps | |

Sure	*definitely*
Pretty sure	
Not as sure	

3 Put the words in the correct order to make sentences.

1. will / planes / fly / Robots / probably / .

   Robots will probably fly planes.

2. future / we / use / Perhaps / in / won't / the / paper / .

   _____

3. our / Robots / houses / certainly / will / clean / .

   _____

4. have / our / clothes / them / will / touch screens / Maybe / in / .

   _____

5. company / I'll / for / software / work / a / definitely / .

   _____

4 Answer the questions using *will* and *won't* to predict the future. Use adverbs of possibility.

1. What will cars do in the future?

   They'll definitely drive themselves.

2. How will we use robots in the future?

   _____

3. Will bikes fly in the future?

   _____

4. Will we have cameras in our jewelry in the future?

   _____

5. How will you be different in the future?

   _____

VOCABULARY Technology verbs

1 Complete the technology verbs.

down	down	down	in	in
✓on	on	out	up	up

1. turn ___on___
2. zoom _____
3. click _____
4. zoom _____
5. back _____
6. sign _____
7. scroll _____
8. sign _____
9. scroll _____
10. shut _____

2 Write the technology verbs from Exercise 1. Some will be pairs of verbs.

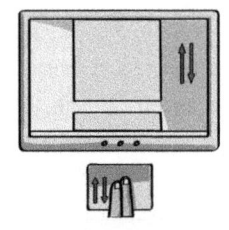

1. ___scroll up___
   ___scroll down___
2. _____
3. _____
4. _____

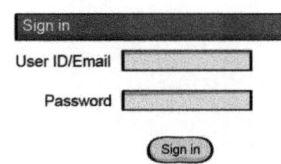

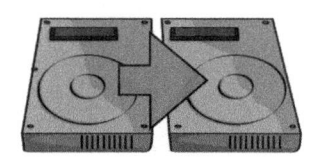

5. _____
6. _____
7. _____

3 Circle the correct technology verbs.

1. Can you **(zoom in)** / **sign out** so we can see it better?
2. Did you **turn on** / **back up** your homework on the flash drive?
3. Don't forget the password or you won't be able to **sign in** / **zoom out**.
4. **Back up** / **Click on** this link to read the blog.
5. **Shut down** / **Scroll up** to look at the picture again.

4 Write sentences. Use technology verbs and your own information.

1. my email
   I never sign out of my email.
2. my school's website
   _____
   _____
3. my computer
   _____
   _____
4. my picture
   _____
   _____
5. my favorite website
   _____
   _____

46 | Unit 7

GRAMMAR First conditional with will (not), may (not), and might (not)

1 Circle the correct words.

1. If her laptop **(breaks)** / **might break**, her parents **buys** / **(might buy)** her a new one.
2. You **won't win** / **won't** the game if you **choose** / **won't choose** that character.
3. If you **get** / **will get** some money, what **you buy** / **will you buy**?
4. You **see** / **will see** it better if you **zoom in** / **might zoom in**.
5. **Will study** / **Will she study** science when she **goes** / **may goes** to college?
6. They **not get** / **may not get** good grades if they **study** / **don't study** harder.

2 Put the words in the correct order to make sentences.

1. of / yours / kind / will / stops / working / you / if / What / phone / get / ?

   What kind of phone will you get if yours stops working?

2. not / don't / get / a / money / tablet / I / I may / save / if / .

   _____

3. the fastest / you / play / new / a / computer / want to / video games, / you / might / need / If / .

   _____

4. back up / may / lose / them / If / our / photos, / we / we / don't / .

   _____

5. video game / make / learns to / kind of / will / he / if he / code / What / write / ?

   _____

3 Correct the sentences.

1. If you click on this link‸you‸see the video.   , will
2. Will you sign into my account if I may give you my password?
3. He may not see the text message if his phone might be off.
4. We not have Wi-Fi if we sit in the library.
5. If you will play the game, first you may not like the movie.
6. How you buy a tablet if you don't save your money?

4 Change the affirmative sentences to negative sentences and the negative sentences to affirmative sentences.

1. You ~~'ll~~ answer your smartphone if you go to the movies.   won't
2. If there are girl characters, I won't play that video game.
3. We'll back up our files if we get a flash drive.
4. If Helen decides to watch a video, she'll choose a comedy.
5. If I post videos, they won't be cat videos.

5 Complete the questions and sentences with will (not), may (not), or might (not) and your own ideas.

1. If I don't do well in computer class,
   I might not get a computer job.
2. What kind of video will you post _____?
3. If I have a blog in the future, _____.
4. Will you buy a _____ if you _____?

Unit 7 | 47

CONVERSATION — Using your cell phone

1 Put the words in order to make questions and answers.

1. do / upload / I / How / a / photo / ?

   How do I upload a photo?

2. need / You / click / to / picture / the / icon / on / .

   _____

3. How / does / touch pad / work / this / ?

   _____

4. you / to / All / do / have / touch / the / is / screen / .

   _____
   _____

2 Complete the sentences.

All you have to	✓ How does it work?
how do I	you need to

Grandmother: Let's take a photo with your smartphone. ¹ *How does it work?*

Boy: First, ² _____ press the round button to turn it on.

Grandmother: Oh, look! There we are. Now, ³ _____ take the picture?

Boy: ⁴ _____ do is press this big button.

Grandmother: And there's our picture. That was easy!

3 Write the questions or answers. Use the phrases and your own ideas.

All you have to	✓ How do I	How do I
How does _____ work?		You need to

1. Ask someone for instructions to send a text.

   How do I send a text?

2. Ask someone how to use a GPS watch.

   _____
   _____

3. Tell someone how to turn on a digital camera.

   _____
   _____

4. Tell someone how to listen to music.

   _____
   _____

5. Ask someone how to watch a video.

   _____
   _____

READING TO WRITE

1 Read the opinion paragraph. Then label the parts: underline the introduction and conclusion. Put a box around the reasons. Circle any facts or examples.

Future Robot Doctors
by Bill Lee

I believe that in the future, when you go to see a doctor, you will see a robot, not a human doctor. One reason I think that is because more and more doctors are using computers to help their patients. The last time I went to a doctor, she used her smartphone to look up what medicine to give me. Another reason I think we will see robots for a cough or cold is that they will give human doctors more time to spend with really sick people. This will save time and money. And another reason is that unlike human doctors, robots don't get sick! If you sneeze on the robot, it won't catch your cold. This way, doctors won't get sick. In conclusion, I think in the future, we will see robot doctors for colds and simple illnesses.

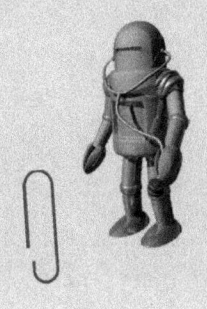

2 Complete the sentences with the opinion and reason phrases. Then number the sentences in order. More than one answer may be possible.

> Another reason is (that)
> For these reasons,
> I think (that)
> In conclusion
> ✓ In my opinion,
> One reason is (that)

_____ _____ people will be able to help each other directly.

_____ _____ people won't need to use money.

_____ _____ we are already doing this, for example with computer code that people share.

_____ _____ we won't need to use money because we will trade everything.

_____ _____ people can easily connect with other people over the Internet. This lets them trade services with each other.

__1__ _In my opinion,_ I believe that in the future, we won't use money.

3 Complete number 1 with an opinion. Complete numbers 2–4 with reasons for that opinion. Complete number 5 with a conclusion. Use your own ideas.

1. In my opinion, _____
   _____
   _____

2. I think (that) _____
   _____
   _____.

3. One reason is (that) _____
   _____
   _____.

4. Another reason is (that) _____
   _____
   _____.

5. For these reasons, _____
   _____
   _____.

Unit 7 | 49

8 The Choices We Make

VOCABULARY Life events

1 Put the letters in the correct order to make life events.

1. OG OT LEGLOCE
   _____

2. TEAK A REYA FOF
   _____

3. GTE ROUY VIRRED'S SINELCE
   _____

4. REETIR
   retire

5. OG OT CLOSOH
   _____

6. EB NOBR
   _____

7. TEG A OJB
   _____

8. NIFHIS OLOHCS
   _____

9. EHVA DHINCELR
   _____

10. ETG ERIDMRA
    _____

2 What are these things? Write the life events from Exercise 1.

1. Before you buy a car, you need to pass a test to do this.
   get your driver's license

2. This is something you do after you've worked for a very long time.
   _____

3. People do this when they are in love and want to be together forever.
   _____

4. You will have teachers when you do this.
   _____

   And you will have professors when you do this.
   _____

5. You will make money when you do this.
   _____

6. This is the first thing you ever do.
   _____

3 Complete the sentences. Use forms of the words from Exercise 1.

1. Julian's grandfather ___retired___ from his job. He worked at the school for 30 years.

2. Tim's little brother is excited because he's finally old enough to _____.

3. First, you _____, and every year after that, you celebrate your birthday.

4. If my mom _____ at the mall, she'll need to _____ and buy a car because it's too far to walk.

5. After she _____ in June, she wants to _____ and travel before she _____.

50 | Unit 8

GRAMMAR be going to and will

1 Choose the correct words.

1. Use **be going to** / **will** to talk about plans in the future.
2. Use **be going to** / **will** to talk about predictions and unplanned decisions.
3. What is he **to do** / **going to do**?
   He is going **to play** / **play** basketball.
   He isn't going **do** / **to do** his homework.
4. Where will she travel first?
   She'll travel / **She travel** to China first.
   She not travel / **She won't travel** to China first.
5. Is he going **study** / **to study** biology?
   Yes, he is. / **Yes, he study.**
   No, he's not going. / **No, he isn't.**
6. **Going to** / **Will** they get married?
   Yes, they **will** / **going to**.
   No, they **aren't going to** / **won't**.

2 Complete the conversation with be going to or will.

Jody: Hi, Scott. Congratulations on finishing school!

Scott: Thanks! You, too. What ¹___are___ you ___going to___ do now?

Jody: I ²_____ go to college in the fall. I got into the Art Academy.

Scott: ³_____ you _____ study art?

Jody: Not exactly. I ⁴_____ study animation.

Scott: That's great.

Jody: What about you? What ⁵_____ you _____ do?

Scott: I'm not sure yet. Maybe I ⁶_____ take a year off and travel.

Jody: That sounds exciting.

Scott: Yeah, but my dad wants me to get a job at his company. I ⁷_____ probably travel in the summer and work in the fall.

3 Unscramble the sentences and questions.

1. probably / you / won't / He / listen / to / .
   He probably won't listen to you.

2. won't / thinks / after-school / get / she / job / She / an / .
   _____
   _____

3. year / off / they'll / take / Maybe / a / .
   _____

4. Australia / will / to / When / travel / Jack / ?
   _____

4 Complete the questions with be going to or will. Then answer the questions with your own information.

1. When ___will___ you finish school?
   _____

2. When _____ you get your driver's license?
   _____

3. Where _____ you live in 10 years?
   _____

4. Is your friend _____ go to college with you?
   _____

5. Are you _____ get married soon?
   _____

VOCABULARY Containers and materials

1 What materials are they made of? Write the container words in the chart.

1. Plastic
   bottle
   _____

2. Paper and cardboard
   _____
   _____

3. Glass
   _____
   _____

4. Cloth
   _____

5. Metal
   _____

2 Circle the correct words.

1. We bring our groceries home in a **(cloth bag)** / **metal can**.

2. At the supermarket, we put the apples in a **glass jar** / **paper bag**.

3. Shampoo comes in a **plastic bottle** / **cardboard box**.

4. My mother bought a **plastic carton** / **cloth bag** of orange juice.

5. I recycled the **glass jar** / **cardboard box** that my new shoes came in.

6. If you wash the **glass jar** / **metal can** the peanut butter came in, you can use it again.

7. I prefer to drink soda from a **cloth bag** / **glass bottle**, not a **cloth bag** / **metal can**.

3 Use container words and your own information to write sentences.

1. (recycle / cardboard box)
   We recycle cardboard boxes at my house.

2. (reuse / cloth bag)
   _____
   _____

3. (not / paper bag)
   _____
   _____

4. (metal can)
   _____
   _____

5. (plastic carton)
   _____
   _____

GRAMMAR Present continuous and simple present for future

1 Put the words in the correct order to ask questions. Use contractions if possible. Then match the questions with the answers.

1. helping / the / they / dolphins / Are / ?
   Are they helping the dolphins? _b_
2. hour / the / Does / leave / bus / in / an / ?
   _____ ___
3. Ben / is / Why / making / video / a / ?
   _____ ___
4. they / have / the / When / meeting / do / ?
   _____ ___
5. plastic / are / collecting / How / they / the / ?
   _____ ___
6. to / do / go / you / When / Japan / ?
   _____ ___

a. They're using a bucket.
b. Yes, they are.
c. I go next month.
d. No, it doesn't.
e. He's teaching people about dolphins.
f. They have the meeting next Saturday.

2 Complete the sentences with the present continuous or simple present.

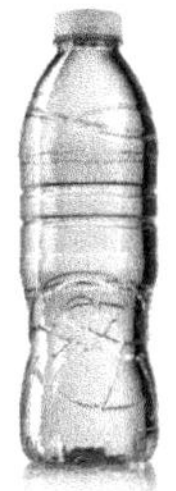

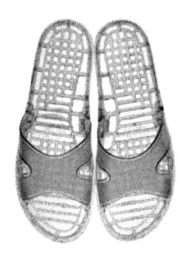

1. I _'m buying_ shoes made from recycled plastic bottles. (buy)
2. The plastic bag recycling drive _____ on June 3. (end)
3. Our town _____ a recycling program. (start)
4. At what time on Tuesday _____ he _____ for Costa Rica? (leave)
5. They _____ to school. (not drive)

3 Use the information in the invitation to complete the questions and answers with the present continuous or simple present.

Who?	You are invited to Kim's birthday party!
What?	Celebrate Kim's birthday. No need to buy gifts. We'll make them!
How?	Collect plastic bags, paper bags, and cardboard from your home and bring them to the party. We'll learn how to recycle them into fun gifts.
Where?	The Art of Recycling Center
When?	Saturday, October 12, at noon
	Be green!
	Ride your bike or take the bus.

1. _Does_ the party _start_ at noon? (start)
   Yes, it does.
2. Where _____ you _____ on Saturday? (go)
   _____
3. _____ you _____ gifts? (buy)
   _____
4. What _____ you _____ from home? (bring)
   _____
5. What _____ you _____ at The Art of Recycling Center? (learn to do)
   _____

4 Answer the questions with the simple present or present continuous and your own information.

1. Are you going to recycle anything next week?
   Yes, I am.
2. When does your family recycle things?
   _____
3. What things are you going to reuse?
   _____
4. What does your family _not_ recycle?
   _____

CONVERSATION: I'm going to get a degree.

1 Complete the conversation.

Absolutely!	✓ I think
I disagree.	Maybe, but I think
I suppose you're right.	

Ingrid: Well, that was an interesting assignment!

Ted: A paper about "What I plan to do after I finish school"? That's easy!

Ingrid: You think so? What *are* you going to do after you finish school?

Ted: I want to study marine biology and the environment. Then I'm going to get a job that helps the ocean. [1] _I think_ it's the most important part of the planet.

Ingrid: [2] _____ people are the most important part of the planet.

Ted: People? [3] _____ People cause the pollution!

Ingrid: [4] _____ That's why the most important thing we can do is change how people do things.

Ted: Hmm. I hadn't thought of it that way. [5] _____ So what are you going to after you finish school?

Ingrid: I'm going to study environmental law!

Ted: Cool! Maybe we can work together.

2 Write a response that agrees or disagrees with each statement. Use the words in the box and your own ideas.

Absolutely!
I disagree.
I suppose you're right.
Maybe, but I think

1. Everyone should study a foreign language.
   _____
   _____

2. I don't think people should eat meat.
   _____
   _____

3. I think everyone should get married.
   _____
   _____

4. I think everyone should have 10 children.
   _____
   _____

5. I think it might be fun to be the leader of a country.
   _____
   _____

READING TO WRITE

To: Ashley Morrison
From: Ben Smith
Subject: Summer Volunteer Opportunity

Dear Ms. Morrison,

I am interested in volunteering at the Senior Center this summer.

I'd like to be a scientist and work with animals someday. I train dogs to be "service dogs." Service dogs help people who can't see or hear well. I train the dogs to visit with people. I think service dogs help people to feel better.

I want to help older people. My grandfather is sick, and I help him. I bring my service dog when I visit my grandfather. It really cheers him up. He is doing much better now.

I have a very well-trained dog named Max, and I'd like to bring him to the Senior Center to visit the older people. I'd volunteer by myself, but I'd rather bring Max with me. Thank you for considering us for the volunteer position.

Sincerely,

Ben (and Max the dog)

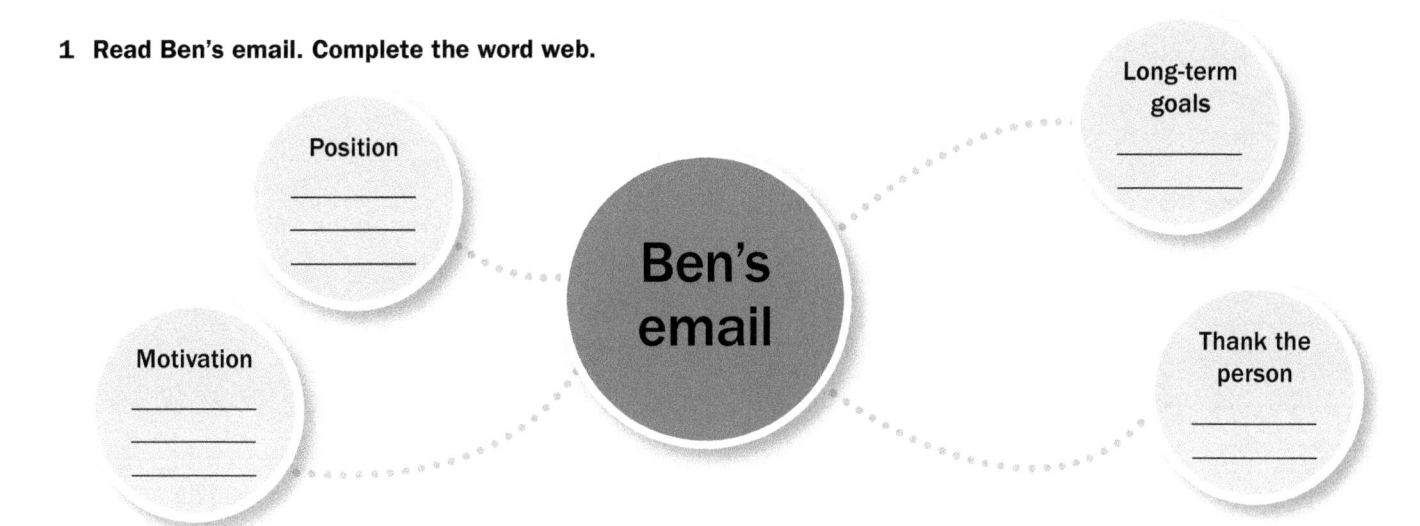

1 Read Ben's email. Complete the word web.

- Position
- Long-term goals
- Motivation
- Thank the person

Ben's email

2 Circle examples of *want*, *would like (to)*, and *would rather ('d rather)* in Ben's email.

3 Complete the sentences using *want*, *would like (to)*, and *would rather ('d rather)*. Use contractions. More than one answer may be possible.

1. She wants to be a doctor. She 'd like to work with children.
2. He _____ volunteer at the recycling center. He'd like to help people learn about recycling.
3. Ken wants to work outdoors. He _____ work in a park than an office.
4. Jillian and Bob _____ help people to lose weight.
5. Paula _____ help sea turtles. She _____ start a volunteer program at the beach than join one online.

Unit 8 | 55

REVIEW UNITS 7–8

1 Label each object. Then underline the materials words, circle the container words, and draw a box around the computer words.

a cardboard box	a metal can
a cloth bag	a paper bag
a glass bottle	a plastic carton
a keyboard	a touch pad
a flash drive	Wi-Fi

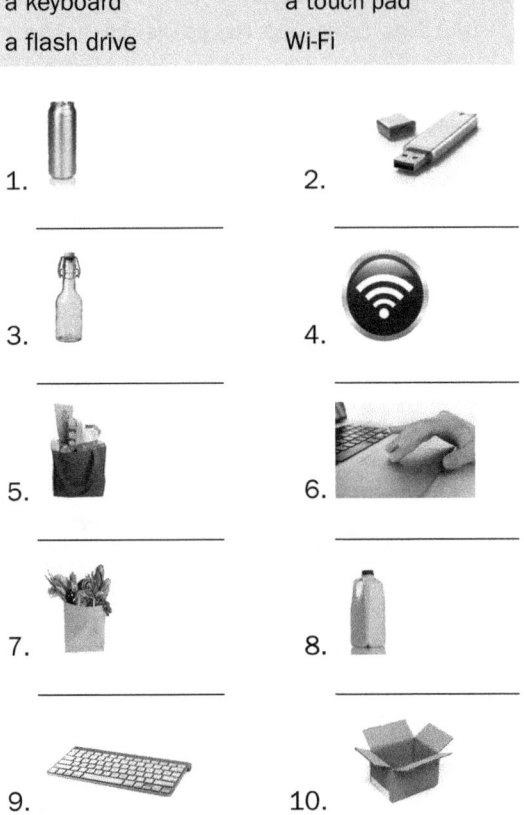

1. _____
2. _____
3. _____
4. _____
5. _____
6. _____
7. _____
8. _____
9. _____
10. _____

2 Complete the conversation with the words in the box.

Click on	sign in
finished school	smartphone
going to college	tablet
How do I	take a year off
printer	You need to

Hannah: My sister just ¹_____. We had a big party. Want to see some photos? I have them on my ²_____.

Stella: Sure. But let's use my ³_____. The screen is bigger.

Hannah: Good idea. Where do I ⁴_____ to the website?

Stella: ⁵_____ this button.

Hannah: OK. Here they are.

Stella: Nice. She got a lot of gifts! Why is she holding that T-shirt?

Hannah: It's where she's ⁶_____ next year.

Stella: Isn't she going this fall?

Hannah: No, she isn't. She's going to ⁷_____. She wants to volunteer in the rainforest in Costa Rica.

Stella: Wow. That's far away.

Hannah: I can show you where she will be on this map. ⁸_____ zoom in?

Stella: ⁹_____ move your fingers like this.

Hannah: Thanks. Here's the website.

3 Write sentences in the future tense with *will* or *won't*.

1. We don't need a keyboard or mouse. (probably)

   _____

2. Computers think like humans. (perhaps)

   _____

3. Clothing and jewelry have touchscreen technology in them. (maybe)

   _____

4. My sister doesn't turn in printed papers for school. (definitely)

   _____

5. I don't go anywhere without my smartphone. (certainly)

   _____

4 Match the phrases to make sentences and questions.

1. If I make a video in the future, _____
2. What will he do _____
3. My friends may not be happy _____
4. If you buy a new smartphone, _____
5. He won't lose his files _____

a. if he backs them up regularly.
b. if I write about them on my blog.
c. which one will you buy?
d. if his smartphone breaks?
e. it won't be a cat video.

5 Answer the questions about Danielle's email (on the right) using *be going to* and *will*.

1. What's Danielle going to do after finishing school?
   _____
   _____
2. Who might she live with?
   _____
   _____
3. Where will she go first?
   _____
   _____
4. How will she get money to travel?
   _____
   _____
5. What is she going to study in college?
   _____
   _____

To: carla_g
From: danigarcia
Subject: I miss you!

Dear Aunt Carla,

How are things in Argentina? I miss you! I'm going to take a year off when I finish school. I'm not going to start college right away. I think it's important to travel and see the world. Mom disagrees with me, though. She wants me to start college right away. But I'd rather travel and learn languages and meet new people. If I save money from my after-school job, I might be able to travel for a year.

If your invitation is still open, would you like a visitor? I'd like to visit you in Argentina to start my year off. I won't stay too long. Mom said that maybe I can help in your restaurant. I'd really like that because I want to study hospitality. What do you think of my plan?

Love,

Daniela

6 Agree or disagree with the following statements. Use your own ideas. Give reasons for your opinions.

Absolutely!   I disagree.   I suppose you're right.

1. In the future, you'll probably have a flying car.
   _____
   _____
2. In the future, you'll definitely be rich and famous.
   _____
   _____
3. In the future, you're probably going to live in your hometown.
   _____
   _____
4. In the future, you're going to retire at age 30.
   _____
   _____

9 Watch Out!

VOCABULARY Accident and injury verbs

1 Find nine more words for accidents and injuries.

✓ bang	burn	cut	hurt	sprain
break	crash	fall off	slip	trip

O	Q	F	A	L	L	O	F	F
J	Y	Z	B	A	N	G	D	N
U	H	U	R	T	T	R	I	P
I	U	S	L	I	P	P	Y	M
S	P	R	A	I	N	S	E	Q
K	G	P	W	W	J	N	Y	M
H	Y	J	E	B	U	R	N	H
V	C	U	T	B	R	E	A	K
Q	G	Y	Z	C	R	A	S	H

2 Label the pictures with the words from Exercise 1.

1. _fall off_
2. _____ 
3. _____ 
4. _____ 
5. _____ 
6. _____ 
7. _____ 
8. _____ 
9. _____ 
10. _____ 

3 Complete the article with the accidents and injuries words from Exercise 1.

It's difficult being a teen. Teens often ¹ _crash_ their bikes and get injured playing sports. But did you know that injuries happen to people over age 65, too? The number one injury might surprise you:

Falling down

Older people often ² _____ down in the kitchen or on the stairs. They might ³ _____ on the stairs or ⁴ _____ on a wet kitchen floor. Twisting an ankle when falling down is one way people can ⁵ _____ an ankle. Falling down can ⁶ _____ the back and cause back pain. For older people, falling down can be very serious. Their bones can ⁷ _____ easily, especially their hips.

A fall can create other injuries, too. A person might ⁸ _____ his or her head on something, or even ⁹ _____ it on something sharp. Older people can avoid falling by wearing good shoes and keeping the floor clear of items they can trip over.

GRAMMAR Present perfect statements with regular and irregular verbs

1 Write the past participle of the verbs. Then underline the verbs that are irregular.

Verb	Past participle
1. burn	*burned*
2. live	
3. slip	
4. study	
5. do	
6. fly	
7. lose	
8. take	

2 Complete the chart. Use *has/have* and the past participle of the words to form the present perfect. More than one answer may be possible.

| been | burned | hurt | ✓ sprained |
| broken | happened | seen | tripped |

	Affirmative
Regular	Ken ¹ *has sprained* his finger playing basketball many times. More falling accidents ² _____ to older people.
	Negative
	Tessa ³ _____ on the stairs before. We ⁴ _____ never _____ any food in the oven before.

Irregular	Affirmative
	Ella ⁵ _____ to Bogota twice. More older people ⁶ _____ a hip than younger people.
	Negative
	Mark ⁷ _____ his back before. We ⁸ _____ our team win before.

3 Write the present perfect affirmative (✓) and negative (✗) statements using the verbs from Exercise 1.

1. I _haven't burned_ my fingers on a hot stove in months. (✗)
2. My team _____ more games than we have won. (✓)
3. Elizabeth _____ for the test. (✓)
4. We _____ dangerous things like this before. (✗)
5. Jack _____ in a helicopter before. (✗)
6. I _____ in this town for a long time. (✓)
7. They _____ the same bus to school for years. (✓)
8. Pete _____ on the ice during a hockey game before. (✗)

4 Use these phrases to write affirmative and negative present perfect sentences with your own information.

1. broke my arm

   I've never broken my arm before.

2. fly to Alaska

   _____

3. fall off a bike

   _____

4. sprain an ankle

   _____

5. sing on stage

   _____

VOCABULARY Parts of the body

1 Unscramble the words.

1. OFOT _____foot_____
2. EKEN _____
3. STEO _____
4. RSWIT _____
5. DRSLOHUE _____
6. KELNA _____
7. COHMAST _____
8. KECN _____
9. BOLEW _____

2 Label the pictures with the words from Exercise 1.

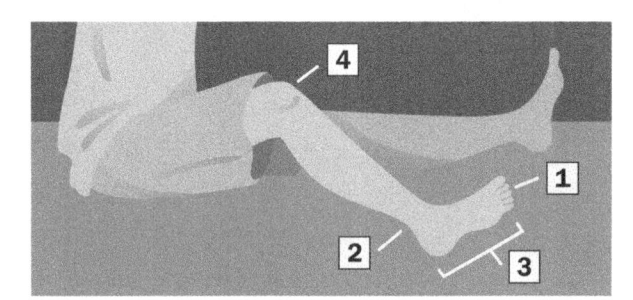

1. _____toes_____ 2. _____
3. _____ 4. _____

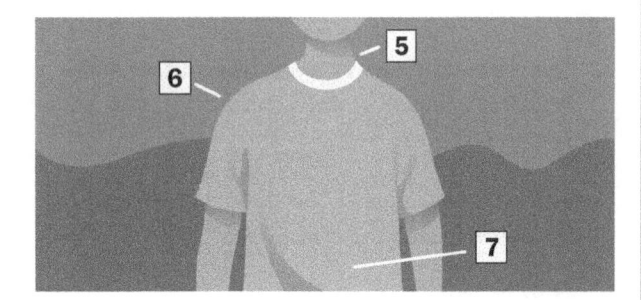

5. _____ 6. _____
7. _____

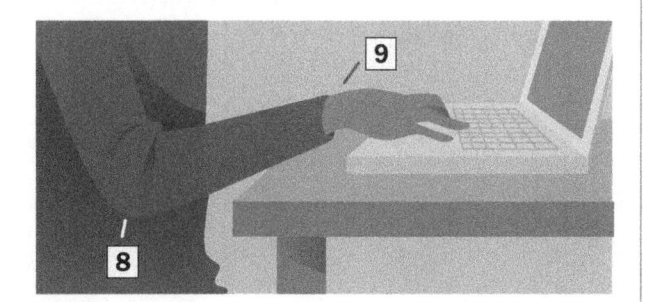

8. _____ 9. _____

3 Complete the sentences with the words from Exercise 1.

1. This is at the top of your arm. ____shoulder____
2. Your head sits on top of this. _____
3. You wear shoes on these. _____
4. You use this to move your foot. _____
5. You can wear a watch or a bracelet on this. _____
6. This is where food goes. _____
7. This is where the leg bends. _____
8. This is where the arm bends. _____
9. You have 10 of these on your foot. _____

4 Complete the conversation.

| ankle | knee | wrist |
| ✓ elbow | shoulder | |

Phillip: Hi, Rita! Hey, what happened to your wrist?

Rita: I was playing volleyball with Olivia last weekend. The ball came over the net, so I jumped up to hit it. But Olivia jumped up at the same time. I bent my arm, and my [1] ___elbow___ hit her on the [2] _____. I'm glad I didn't hit her head. But she fell and twisted her [3] _____ when she landed.

Phillip: Ouch!

Rita: Well, it gets worse. Olivia couldn't stand up at all! I went over to help her, but I slipped and fell. And I bent my [4] _____ too far when I landed on my hand. I think it's sprained. We're going to miss several volleyball games.

Phillip: I know how you feel. I was running during soccer practice and fell. I landed on my [5] _____. It really hurts to bend my leg now.

Rita: I guess we'll just have to *watch* our games for now!

GRAMMAR Present perfect questions; present perfect vs. simple past

1 Match the questions with the correct answers.

1. Why has he had so many accidents? — c. Because he's clumsy.
2. Has she ever fallen down the stairs? — a. No, she hasn't.
3. What happened on your vacation? — d. I tripped and fell. I hurt my wrist.
4. What bones have you broken? — f. My arm and my finger.
5. Have you ever banged your head? — b. Yes, I have.
6. Have you ever sprained your ankle? — e. Yes, I have. I sprained it yesterday.

2 Complete the questions in the present perfect.

1. A: _Have_ you _ever gone_ windsurfing? (ever, go)
   B: No, we haven't.
2. A: _____ you _____ in a helicopter? (ever, ride)
   B: Yes, I have. I rode in one last week.
3. A: _____ they _____ Portuguese? (ever, study)
   B: Yes, they have.
4. A: Where _____ you _____? (live)
   B: In Guadalajara and New York.
5. A: Why _____ he _____ the bus every day this week? (take)
   B: Because his bike is broken.
6. A: _____ she _____ a video? (ever, make)
   B: No, she hasn't.

3 Use the chart to write the questions and answers.

Who?	Doing what?	How?	What injury?	When?
Kate	dancing	trip	sprain ankle	in the past
George	biking	fall	none	never
Stacey	hockey	slip	broken wrist	last winter
Brian	car accident	crash	hurt neck	last May
Maria	surfing	fall off	hurt shoulder	on vacation

1. _Has_ Kate _ever sprained_ her ankle?
   Yes, she _has_.
2. _____ George _____ off his bike?
   No, he _____.
3. Stacey, _____ you _____ playing hockey?
   Yes, I _____.
   When?
   _____.
4. Brian, what _____ last May?
   _____
5. Maria, _____ you _____ off your surfboard?
   _____
   What _____?
   _____

4 Answer the questions with your own information. Write complete sentences.

1. Have you ever lost your backpack?
   Yes, I have. I lost it last week.
2. Have you ever broken any bones?
   _____
   _____
3. Have you ever tried to surf?
   _____
   _____
4. Have you ever traveled to another country?
   _____
   _____
5. What good books have you read?
   _____
   _____

CONVERSATION Good news, bad news

1 Complete the conversation with the words to react to good news and bad news.

✓ I'm sorry to hear that.	That's cool!
That sounds like fun.	that's too bad

Emily: Hi, Zack. How was your camping trip?

Zack: It was good and bad, I guess. First, the bad news – Jim climbed a tree, fell out of the tree, and landed in the fire!

Emily: Oh no! ¹ *I'm sorry to hear that.* Is he OK?

Zack: He's fine, but he burned part of his shoe.

Emily: Oh, ² _____ about the shoe.

Zack: I know. But it gets better . . . I took a video of him falling out of the tree and put it on my website. It's gotten more than 10,000 views so far.

Emily: ³ _____

Zack: Yeah! It is! And the local news heard about it. So we are going to be on TV.

Emily: Wow! ⁴ _____

2 Correct the reactions. Mark (✓) if the reaction is correct. Use the expressions from Exercise 1.

1. **A:** I'm going to Hawaii for vacation!
   B: ~~I'm sorry to hear that~~.
   That sounds like fun.

2. **A:** I'm sorry I can't come to your party on Saturday.
   B: That's cool.
   _____

3. **A:** My bike was stolen yesterday.
   B: That's too bad.
   _____

4. **A:** I made a new friend in guitar class.
   B: I'm sorry to hear that.
   _____

5. **A:** She broke her arm skateboarding.
   B: That's cool.
   _____

3 Write a reaction to each sentence. Use the phrases from Exercise 1.

1. **A:** My pet turtle died.
   B: _____

2. **A:** I won the skateboard competition!
   B: _____

3. **A:** We are going to the swimming pool this weekend.
   B: _____

4. **A:** I can't go to the movie tonight because I have to do homework.
   B: _____

READING TO WRITE

1 Number the paragraphs to put the parts of the email in the correct order.

To: Adriana S.
From: Laurel M.
Subject: Party invitation

Hi Adriana,

___ We're going to take her to Donner Lake. She used to sail there when she was a girl. So, my Dad rented a sailboat to take her out. She doesn't know about it yet. It's a surprise!

___ Again, I'm really sorry. Have a great time! Text me some pictures. Maybe we can go to a concert together next month.

___ I'd love to come, but I can't go with you.

_1_ Thanks for inviting me to the concert on Saturday.

___ It's my grandmother's birthday. She's going to be 70. We're spending the weekend with her.

Your friend,

Laurel

2 Read the email again. Answer the questions. Write complete sentences.

1. What phrase does Laurel use to thank Adriana for the invitation?

   Thanks for inviting me

2. What phrases does Laurel use to apologize?

   _____
   _____

3. What is Laurel's reason for not going?

   _____
   _____

4. What suggestion does Laurel make at the end?

   _____
   _____

5. What two places does Laurel apologize in?

   _____
   _____

3 Write sentences to refuse an invitation to go to the beach. Use phrases from Exercises 1 and 2.

A: Can you come to the beach on Saturday?

1. Thank the person for the invitation:

   B: _____
   _____

2. Apologize and refuse:

   B: _____
   _____

3. Explain why you can't go:

   B: _____
   _____

4. Suggest another time:

   B: _____
   _____

Unit 9 | 63

10 Have Fun!

VOCABULARY Free-time activities

1 Complete the free-time activity phrases.

celebrate	✓play
go	play
hang out	read
have	spend
listen	take

1. _play_ video games
2. _____ photos
3. _____ a party
4. _____ your birthday
5. _____ books
6. _____ with friends
7. _____ time with your family
8. _____ an instrument
9. _____ to music
10. _____ to a dance

2 Complete the paragraphs. Use the verbs from Exercise 1.

1. When you _celebrate_ your birthday, you _____ with your family, like your grandparents and cousins. You eat cake and open presents. Your parents always _____ photos when you blow out the candles on the cake.

2. My favorite things to do when I _____ with friends? That's easy. We like to _____ video games. We can play them for hours. And we often _____ to music, too.

3. My brother is very friendly. He doesn't like to spend time alone. His favorite thing to do is _____ to a dance at school. If my parents would let him, he'd _____ a dance party at our house!

4. My friend Carol is very quiet and spends a lot of time alone. She likes to _____ books. She also likes to _____ instruments. She is learning to play the drums. Maybe she won't be quiet any more!

3 Complete the chart with the activities from Exercise 1 and your own information. Then write sentences.

Activity	When?	Where?	Who?
1. hang out with friends	last weekend	sports park	Bill, Lisa
2. spend time with family			
3. celebrate birthday			
4. _____			
5. _____			

1. _I hung out with my friends Bill and Lisa last weekend. We went to the sports park._
2. _____
3. _____
4. _____
5. _____

GRAMMAR Indefinite pronouns

1 Label the graphs with indefinite pronouns.

anyone	no one
anything	nothing
anywhere	nowhere
✓everyone	someone
everything	something
everywhere	somewhere

PEOPLE

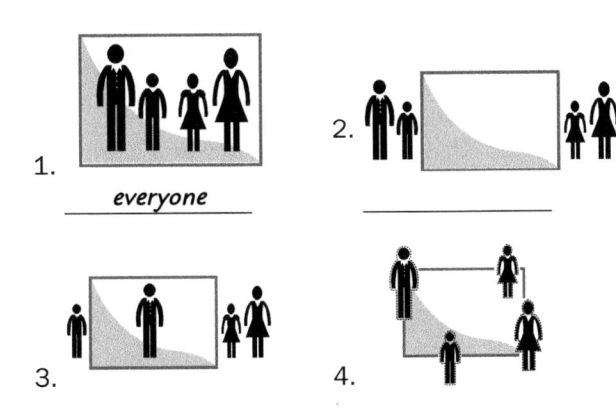

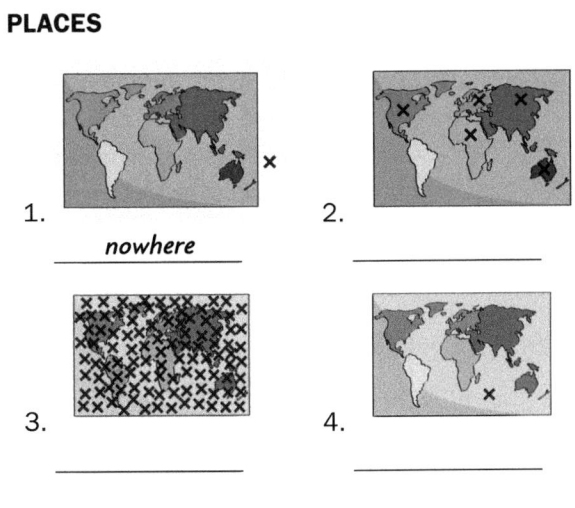

1. _everyone_
2. _____
3. _____
4. _____

PLACES

1. _nowhere_
2. _____
3. _____
4. _____

THINGS

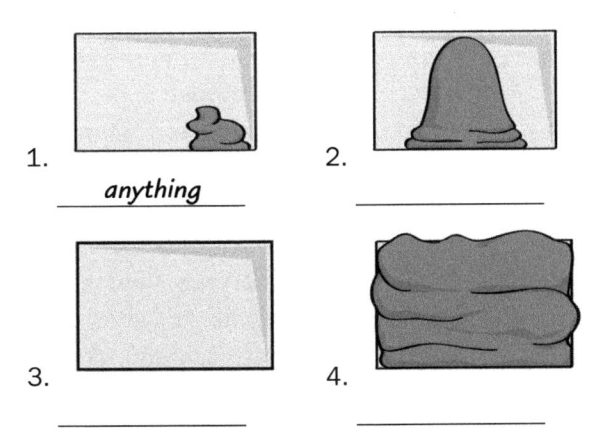

1. _anything_
2. _____
3. _____
4. _____

2 Complete the sentences with indefinite pronouns.

anyone	everywhere
anything	No one
✓everything	something

1. The food was delicious. He's eaten ___everything___ on his plate.

2. It's polite to bring _____ when you are invited to dinner.

3. Don't speak if you don't have _____ nice to say.

4. He can't remember _____'s name.

5. His passport is full of stamps because he's traveled _____.

6. _____ answered the last question correctly.

3 Correct the negative sentences. Mark ✓ if the sentence is correct.

1. I didn't go ~~nowhere~~ _anywhere_ fun on my birthday. _____

2. He didn't know no one at the party. _____

3. I don't know someone who loves football more than me. _____

4. Julie didn't do everything exciting on vacation. _____

5. Everyone goes to the free concerts in the park. _____

6. There is always anything to do at the city center. _____

Unit 10 | 65

VOCABULARY Adjectives of feeling

1 Use the pictures to complete the crossword.

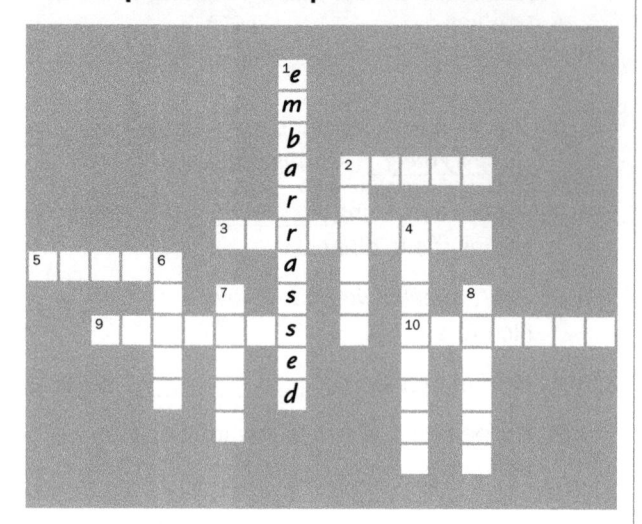

ACROSS

2. _____
3. _____ 
5. _____ 
9. _____ 
10. _____ 

DOWN

1. *embarrassed*
2. _____ 
4. _____ 
6. _____ 
7. _____ 
8. _____ 

2 Choose the correct words.

Scott: Hi, Ernie! Tell me about your camping trip with your brother.

Ernie: It was my first time camping. So I was ¹**embarrassed /(excited)** I guess I was also a little ²**nervous / upset** because anything could be out there in the woods, you know?

Scott: You're ³**scared / tired** of bears, aren't you?

Ernie: Yes! I am very ⁴**afraid / bored** of them. So, anyway, I was in my tent about to fall asleep, and I heard a noise outside. It was coming closer. My heart started beating very fast. I felt ⁵**embarrassed / stressed**. After a minute, I peeked out of the tent.

Scott: What was there?

Ernie: Something furry landed in front of my tent! I screamed. Then I heard my brother laughing. He threw his furry hat in front of the tent to scare me!

Scott: You must have really been ⁶**excited / surprised**.

Ernie: For a moment I was. Then my brother said he was ⁷**bored / nervous**, so he thought it would be fun to scare me. That made me ⁸**afraid / angry**. Then I was ⁹**embarrassed / surprised** that I screamed because the people in the next campsite heard me. And then I was ¹⁰**nervous / upset** with my brother for teasing me. I couldn't sleep all night. Now, I'm just ¹¹**scared / tired**.

Scott: That's kind of a funny story, you know.

Ernie: *Now* it is!

GRAMMAR too and enough

1 Circle the correct words to complete the rules.

1. Use **enough** / **too + adjective** / **infinitive + infinitive** to show something is more than what we want or need.

2. Use **adjective + enough + infinitive** / **infinitive + enough / too + infinitive** to show something is what we want or need.

3. **Not + adjective** / **Not enough** / **Too + adjective** shows something is less than or more than what we want or need.

2 Complete the chart with *too* and *enough*.

	More than	What we want	Less than
tall	too tall	tall enough	not tall enough
warm			
brave			
nervous			
young			

3 Put the words in the correct order to make sentences.

1. ending / The / enough / wasn't / movie's / surprising / .

   The movie's ending wasn't surprising enough.

2. to / race / the / Bill / enough / wasn't / win / fast / .

   _____

3. home / was / sick / stay / Becky / enough / to / .

   _____

4. wasn't / He / nervous / too / to / remember / the / answer / .

   _____

5. it / They / talk / too / were / to / upset / about / .

   _____

6. spider / too / speak / was / when / he / Bob / saw / to / the / scared / .

   _____

4 Circle the correct words.

1. The boy is **too short** / **n't short enough** to ride the bike.

2. He was **too afraid** / **n't afraid enough** to answer the door.

3. The team was **too strong** / **n't strong enough** to win the game.

4. She was **too tired** / **n't tired enough** to finish her homework.

5. The tea is **too hot** / **n't hot enough** to drink. You might burn your mouth.

5 Complete the sentences with your own information.

1. I'm (not) old enough to ___*drive a car*___.

2. I'm (not) too scared to _____.

3. I'm (not) brave enough to _____.

4. I'm (not) interested enough to _____.

5. Climbing a mountain is (not) something I'm _____.

6. Acting in a movie is (not) something I'm _____.

Unit 10 | 67

CONVERSATION Birthday plans

1 Match the suggestions with the responses.

1. Why don't we try surfing?
2. I want to see the new zombie movie.
3. Why don't we go shopping?
4. How about watching the skateboarders?
5. Why don't we go swimming?
6. How about calling our friends to join us?

a. That's a great idea! Luckily, I brought my bathing suit.
b. I'd rather watch the surfers. They're more exciting.
c. I'm too scared to try that. I'd rather go swimming.
d. That's a great idea! I heard it's really good.
e. That's a great idea! You call Jorge, and I'll call Kaitlin.
f. I'd rather be outside than in a mall. Maybe we can do that tonight.

2 Choose the correct suggestion or response.

1. **A:** Why don't we go see that new horror movie?
   B: I don't like horror movies. **That's a great idea!** / **I'd rather see the new action movie.** *(circled)*

2. **A:** It's a nice day. How about we go for a walk?
   B: **I'd rather go for a walk. / That's a great idea!**

3. **A:** We haven't seen our cousins in a while. **How about we stay home? / Why don't we visit them?**
   B: That's a great idea!

3 Complete the conversations with your own ideas. Use the phrases in the box.

| How about | That's a great idea |
| I'd rather | Why don't we |

1. **A:** Let's go skiing.
   B: It's too cold. _Why don't we go to the movies?_

2. **A:** _____ go skiing?
   B: There's not enough snow.
   _____
   _____

3. **A:** _____ playing video games?
   B: It's too nice outside.
   _____
   _____

4. **A:** _____ studying for the test this afternoon?
   B: _____
   _____

5. **A:** _____ go to the museum?
   B: _____
   _____

68 | Unit 10

READING TO WRITE

1 Read the email and complete the chart.

To: Raquel
From: Paul
Subject: Let's go power-kiting!

Hey Raquel,

How are you? I saw your windsurfing photos online. There were some good <u>ones</u>!

I'm having a party this weekend, and you're invited. It's a party to introduce my friends to the sport of power-kiting. It's like skateboarding with a kite. We're going to try it at the park. I don't know if you've tried power-kiting before, but I think you'll like it because you like wind sports. I tried it last weekend, and it is easier than it looks.

We'll meet at the skate park at noon on Saturday. Then after we power-kite for a couple hours, we'll go to Rocky's for pizza. If you can't join us for power-kiting, you can meet us there.

Let me know by Thursday if you can join us. I need to let the park know by then how many people are coming.

Your friend,

Paul

Paul's Party	
1. What is the event?	*power-kiting party*
2. What is the reason for the event?	
3. When is the event?	
4. Where is the event?	
5. What are the activities?	
6. What response does Paul ask for?	

2 Read the email again. Underline the referencing words *ones*, *It*, *there*, and *then*. Then draw a line from the referencing word to the noun it refers to.

3 Complete the sentences with the correct reference words.

1. I have a lot of good friends. I have a lot of fun with _____them_____.

2. Why don't we go downtown on Saturday afternoon? Are you free _____?

3. How about coming to the concert with me tonight? I think you'll really like _____.

4. Are you learning to play the guitar? How is _____ going?

5. Why don't we spend some time with your cousins? I really like hanging out with _____.

6. I would like to go to the movie with you tomorrow, but I'm busy _____.

REVIEW UNITS 9–10

1 Look at the pictures. Circle the correct answers.

Ken: I fell playing ice hockey last winter, and I ¹**broke / fell off** my ²**ankle / shoulder**. Then I couldn't walk. While it was healing, I sat on the sofa a lot and ³**went dancing / spent time with my family**. They gave me a camera so I wouldn't be ⁴**bored / nervous**. That's when I started to ⁵**play an instrument / take photos**. I was ⁶**stressed / surprised** how much I liked it.

Emma: I love to ⁷**celebrate my birthday / read books**. This year, we had a big party at my house. There were candles on the cake, and they ⁸**burned / sprained** the paper on one of my gifts! I ate too much cake, and my ⁹**elbow broke / stomach hurt**. It was fun to ¹⁰**have a party / play video games**, but I was ¹¹**stressed / tired** afterwards.

Roger: Last summer, I was mountain biking, and I ¹²**crashed / sprained**. I ¹³**fell off / hurt** and ¹⁴**banged / slipped** my knee. I couldn't walk for a while. I thought I would play video games, but my mom said I should ¹⁵**have a party / play an instrument**. That's why I started to learn the guitar.

2 Match the actions with the feelings.

1. Jackie slipped on the floor in the cafeteria.
2. Bill fell asleep in school.
3. Pam didn't like playing video games.
4. Alex played the violin in his first concert.
5. Anna had to read a lot of books for her test.

a. He was nervous.
b. She was bored.
c. She was embarrassed.
d. She was stressed.
e. He was tired.

3 Circle the correct answers.

1. Have you ever broken a toe?
   a. Yes, she has.
   b. No, I haven't.
2. What bones have you broken?
   a. Yes, I have.
   b. My arm and a finger.
3. Has he ever gone power-kiting?
   a. Yes, he has.
   b. He slipped yesterday.
4. What happened when Mike fell off his bike?
   a. He sprained his arm.
   b. No, he hasn't.
5. Have they ever lost a game?
   a. Yes. They lost one last week.
   b. Yes, I have.

4 Circle the correct answers.

1. I don't see any_____ to buy in this store.
   a. -one   b. -thing   c. -where
2. I've looked every_____ for the cat.
   a. -one   b. -thing   c. -where
3. I don't think any_____ could surf those waves.
   a. -one   b. -thing   c. -where
4. There's _____ who can come on Saturday.
   a. anyone   b. everyone   c. no one

5 Write questions and answers with the present perfect or the simple past.

1. Millie / crash her bike / ever (yes, last month)

   Q: _____
   A: _____

2. Paula / go kite-surfing / before (no, power-kiting)

   Q: _____
   A: _____

3. Stefan / live Madrid / ever (no, Buenos Aires, last year)

   Q: _____
   A: _____

4. You / study English / ever (yes, two years ago)

   Q: _____
   A: _____

6 Rewrite the sentences to make them correct.

1. Tom didn't tell no one about the surprise party.

   _____

2. Why have he be late for school every day this week?

   _____
   _____

3. Cara hasn't broke any bones before.

   _____

4. Sam slip at the pool yesterday.

   _____

7 Complete the emails with the correct phrases.

haven't been	sounded like fun
How about	That's a great idea!
I'd rather	Too bad
I'm too scared	Why don't you

To: Dylan
From: Lena
Subject: RE: Invitation

Hi Dylan,

How are you? Thanks for the invitation to go swimming last weekend. I was out of town. We went surfing in Sayulita. Sorry I missed it. It ¹_____.

I'm taking a group of friends sky-diving next weekend. ²_____ coming along? It's not real sky-diving, like jumping out of a plane. It's indoors! You float in the air in a big wind tunnel. It looks cool. I ³_____ sky-diving before. Have you? ⁴_____ join us?

Let me know by Friday if you can make it.

Talk to you later,

Lena

To: Lena
From: Dylan
Subject: RE: RE: Invitation

Hey Lena,

Indoor sky-diving? ⁵_____ ⁶_____ it's the same day as my cousin's birthday party. We're going to a car race. ⁷_____ try sky-diving than go to the race, but only because it's indoors. ⁸_____ to jump out of a plane. But thanks for inviting me.

Maybe we can go skateboarding on Sunday.

See ya!

Dylan

A Cool LIFE

Unit 6 Video 6.1

BEFORE YOU WATCH

1 Look at the picture from the video. Circle the correct words to complete the sentences.

1. This house in Coober Pedy, Australia, is **underground / above ground**.

2. When it is very hot outside, it is **cooler / warmer** in this house.

3. This house needs a lot of **lamps / bedrooms**.

WHILE YOU WATCH

2 Watch the video. Number the sentences 1–5 in the order you see them.

1. Two people walk into a mine. _____
2. People play golf outside at night. _____
3. A woman cooks in her kitchen. _____
4. A woman finds an opal in a mine. _____
5. A man cleans his living room. _____

3 Watch the video again. Look carefully at the rooms in the underground house. Check (✓) what you see, and where.

Object	Living room	Dining room / Kitchen	Bedroom
lamps			
pictures			
beds			
table			
chairs			

AFTER YOU WATCH

4 Work with a partner. What do you do when it is really hot or cold outside – during the day or at night?

> When it's really hot, I swim during the day. At night I read. When it's very cold, I go ice skating during the day. At night, I watch TV.

82 | Unit 6

Moving HOUSE

Unit 6 Video 6.3

BEFORE YOU WATCH

1 Look at the picture from the video and read the text. Then match the words with the definitions.

Joey was looking for a new house. He found a cabin he liked. He put the cabin on logs. He used a bulldozer to pull the cabin to a new place.

1. cabin _____
2. log _____
3. bulldozer _____

a. a big machine that can move things
b. a small wooden house
c. a thick piece of a tree

WHILE YOU WATCH

2 Watch the video. Circle the correct answers.

1. Joey lives in the _____ of Tanana, Alaska.
   a. city   b. town   c. state
2. He lived with his father until _____ ago.
   a. a month   b. a year   c. two years
3. He doesn't have _____ money.
   a. much   b. more   c. some
4. He wanted to live _____ his family and friends.
   a. with   b. next to   c. closer to
5. Joey's _____ move the logs.
   a. brothers   b. cousins   c. friends

3 Watch the video again. Check (✓) the sentences you hear.

1. ❑ Can he buy the house and move?
2. ❑ So first, they must get some logs.
3. ❑ It's really hard work.
4. ❑ I'm very excited!
5. ❑ It's perfect!

AFTER YOU WATCH

4 Work with a partner. Take turns describing your favorite room at home. What does it look like? What do you like to do in it?

> My bedroom is my favorite room. There's a bed and two windows . . . and my computer. I like listening to music in my bedroom.

A Pizza ROBOT

Unit 7 Video 7.1

BEFORE YOU WATCH

1 Look at the picture from the video. Find the words in the puzzle.

customer   deliver   order   pizza   robot

B	O	R	L	C	N	F	R	A	Z
P	I	C	U	S	T	O	M	E	R
A	E	Q	Z	S	P	I	Z	Z	A
R	O	B	O	T	O	T	A	C	I
A	F	R	D	O	X	Z	F	U	B
S	D	H	V	M	K	Z	X	A	O
P	E	J	D	E	L	I	V	E	R
O	R	D	E	R	A	P	B	R	O

WHILE YOU WATCH

2 Watch the video. Circle the correct answers.

1. The men work on _____ in the US.
   a. a lake   b. a river   c. an island
2. The pizza from the blimp is _____.
   a. cold   b. hot   c. delicious
3. One of the men in the robot car is _____.
   a. driving the car b. watching a video c. using a computer
4. The men put _____ on the smaller robot.
   a. glasses   b. clothes   c. a sign
5. One man opens Luigi's _____ with a credit card.
   a. oven   b. box   c. window

3 Watch the video again. Complete the sentences with the correct words.

itself   map   problems   ready   without

1. A robot car drives _____.
2. The car has _____ at first.
3. In the future, robots will use a city _____.
4. Luigi goes around the car _____ a problem.
5. They get a hot pizza _____ to eat.

AFTER YOU WATCH

4 Work with a partner. Discuss: What do you think robots will do for people in the future? Make a list, and then share it with another pair.

> **A:** I think robots will clean houses in the future.
> **B:** I think they'll cook dinner.

Music SHARING

Unit 7 Video 7.3

BEFORE YOU WATCH

1 Look at the picture from the video. Complete the paragraph with the correct words.

| download | industry | sharing | store |

Twenty years ago, people had to buy music from a music ^{1}_____. Then it became possible to ^{2}_____ music files on a computer. This changed the music ^{3}_____. Will file ^{4}_____ be illegal in the future?

WHILE YOU WATCH

2 Watch the video. Are the sentences true (*T*) or false (*F*)? Correct the false sentences.

1. In 1999, it wasn't easy to get music. _____
2. Shawn Fanning created a computer to download songs. _____
3. Soon Napster became a big business. _____
4. Bands got money from Napster for their music. _____
5. Record companies stopped file sharing. _____

3 Watch the video again. Complete the sentences with the words you hear.

1. What part will music _____?
2. In one _____, more than 10,000 people had it.
3. Soon a million _____ had it.
4. So they closed Napster _____.
5. Maybe you will have the _____ big idea!

AFTER YOU WATCH

4 Work in small groups. Discuss: What do people buy online, and what do they buy in a store?

> My parents buy books and DVDs online. They buy food at a store.

A School at HOME

Unit 8 Video 8.1

BEFORE YOU WATCH

1 Look at the pictures from the video. Read the definition. Do you think the sentences are true (*T*) or false (*F*)?

homeschool (verb) to teach your children at home

1. Children in many countries are homeschooled. _____
2. Very few homeschooled students attend a college or university. _____
3. Many homeschooled students are active in their communities. _____
4. Homeschooled students usually learn about only one subject. _____

WHILE YOU WATCH

2 Watch the video. Circle the correct answers.

1. Maggy's **mother / father** helps her on the computer.
2. Her **mother / father** teaches classes at home.
3. The Botros children study science, English, and **math / history**.
4. Maggy **would / wouldn't** like to go to a large school.
5. Maggy wants to be a **teacher / scientist** in the future.

3 Watch the video again. Match the phrases to make true sentences.

1. My oldest son has _____   a. work out for him.
2. School just didn't _____   b. away from home.
3. Maggy is really _____   c. some special needs.
4. Sometimes Maggy studies _____ d. close to her brothers and sisters.

AFTER YOU WATCH

4 Work with a partner. Compare your school to the school in the video. What do you like best about each type of school?

> My class is bigger than the class in the video. I like the small classes in the video. I really like playing soccer at my school.

86 | Unit 8

Time for an ADVENTURE!

BEFORE YOU WATCH Unit 8 Video 8.3

1 Look at the pictures from the video. Match the words with the correct defnitions.

1. chef _____
2. archaeologist _____
3. dinosaur _____
4. volunteer _____

a. an animal that lived on Earth millions of years ago
b. a professional cook
c. someone who chooses to help or do work without getting paid
d. a scientist who studies ancient cultures

WHILE YOU WATCH

2 Watch the video. Check (✔) the sentences you hear.

1. ❑ So I'm taking a year on after high school.
2. ❑ Perhaps I'll go to Siena and work as a volunteer.
3. ❑ It has wide, open spaces and green forests.
4. ❑ Or I'll visit a village and see people my age.
5. ❑ Maybe I'll help an archaeologist look for a T-Rex!

3 Watch the video again. Match the adventures with the places.

1. Rome _____
2. Siena _____
3. South Africa _____
4. Madagascar _____

a. repair old buildings
b. look for dinosaur bones
c. learn to cook
d. help animals

AFTER YOU WATCH

4 Work in small groups. Discuss: What adventures are you going to have when you finish school?

> I'm going to go hiking in the mountains for a week . . . and I'm going to college in a big city. That will be an adventure.

DANGER *in our* FOOD

Unit 9 Video 9.1

BEFORE YOU WATCH

1 Look at the pictures from the video. Do you think the sentences are true (*T*) or false (*F*)?

1. Many people become sick every year from eating bad food.   _____
2. Food that will make you sick usually looks delicious.   _____
3. Water in public places is always safe to drink.   _____
4. Fruits and vegetables are safer to eat than cookies.   _____

WHILE YOU WATCH

2 Watch the video. Complete the sentences with the correct words.

1. Madison was like many _____.
2. Sometimes there is E. coli in food and _____.
3. The _____ are worried.
4. The E. coli was in the _____ dough.
5. _____ was very lucky.

3 Watch the video again. Check (✓) the sentences you hear.

1. ❏ She enjoyed dancing and singing with her friends.
2. ❏ E. coli 0157 is a kind of bacteria.
3. ❏ How did Madison get E. coli?
4. ❏ The doctors taste many different kinds of food.
5. ❏ Soon over 70 people are ill with E. coli.

AFTER YOU WATCH

4 Work in small groups. Discuss: Have you or a family member ever eaten something that made you really sick? What did you eat? What did you feel like?

> I ate some fish a year ago and got really sick. I felt sick to my stomach. I didn't want to eat anything for days.

88 | Unit 9

A DEADLY Job

Unit 9 Video 9.3

BEFORE YOU WATCH

1 Look at the pictures from the video. Label the pictures with the correct words. Then answer the questions.

   crocodile   kangaroo   snake   spider

1. _____   2. _____   3. _____   4. _____

5. Which of these animals are dangerous? _____

6. Which of these animals sometimes live in people's homes? _____

WHILE YOU WATCH

2 Watch the video. Number the snakes 1–5 in the order you see them.

1. a snake in a pantry   _____
2. a snake on a rock   _____
3. a snake in a bag   _____
4. a snake in a box   _____
5. a snake on the floor of a room _____

3 Watch the video again. Circle the correct answers.

1. Adelaide is on the **south / north** coast of Australia.
2. The brown snake is the **most / second most** dangerous snake in the world.
3. Snake-Away takes snakes **to / from** people's homes.
4. The man must hold the snake by its **head / tail**.

AFTER YOU WATCH

4 Work with a partner. What animals or insects live in people's houses? Which are dangerous? Complete the chart.

Animal	Dangerous?
Cat	No
Dog	Sometimes
Ant	

A New York City FOOD TOUR

Unit 10 Video 10.1

BEFORE YOU WATCH

1 Look at the pictures from the video. Complete the sentences with the correct words.

delicatessen   desserts   hot dogs

1. New York City has food from all over the world. You can get a delicious lunch in a _____ like this one.

2. People sell _____ and sandwiches on the streets of New York.

3. Some places only serve _____, like this ice cream sundae.

WHILE YOU WATCH

2 Watch the video. Circle the correct answers.

1. Katz's Delicatessen is the _____ in New York.
   a. largest   b. oldest   c. busiest
2. Sylvia's Restaurant opened in _____.
   a. 1888   b. 1952   c. 1962
3. People go to Serendipity to eat _____.
   a. desserts   b. hot dogs   c. pizza
4. The fudge that people eat at Serendipity is made of _____.
   a. ice   b. cream   c. chocolate

3 Watch the video again. Number the sentences 1–4 in the order you see them.

1. A man in a red T-shirt dancing _____
2. A woman with big earrings eating a sandwich _____
3. A man in a black T-shirt cutting meat _____
4. A group of horses crossing a street _____

AFTER YOU WATCH

4 Where can you go to get great food where you live? Complete the chart below. Share your list with a partner.

For . . .	Place	Great food
Lunch	Rosetta	seafood tacos
Dinner		
Dessert		

Punkin CHUNKIN!

Unit 10 Video 10.3

BEFORE YOU WATCH

1 Read the definitions of the words from the video. Then find the words in the puzzle.

pumpkin (noun) a large, round, orange vegetable

chuck (verb) to throw

launch (verb) to send something into the air

shoot (verb) to cause something to fly or move quickly; to use a gun

U	M	P	O	P	R	L	C
I	A	L	A	U	N	C	H
X	H	W	P	M	Q	Z	S
T	S	H	Z	P	R	E	T
C	H	U	C	K	F	D	O
B	O	A	V	I	H	V	M
H	O	I	N	N	J	O	E
E	T	H	O	T	R	R	R

WHILE YOU WATCH

2 Watch the video. Are the sentences true (*T*) or false (*F*)? Correct the false sentences.

1. Everyone calls this sport a mess. _____
2. People build machines to chuck the pumpkins. _____
3. People come here every two years for this festival. _____
4. Jake works so hard because of his family. _____
5. Jake's father was the world champion. _____

3 Watch the video again. Check (✓) the sentences you hear.

1. ❑ Have you heard about the Punkin Chunkin contest?
2. ❑ Some people say it's a sport.
3. ❑ So why do people do this?
4. ❑ Now the whole family helps shoot pumpkins!
5. ❑ To chuck pumpkins, why else?

AFTER YOU WATCH

4 Work in small groups. Discuss: What are some unusual traditions in your town or country? Does your family have any unusual traditions?

> My family has an unusual tradition for New Year's Eve. At midnight, we break dishes in the kitchen. Then we go outside to plant a tree!

Unit 10 | 91

This page intentionally left blank.

Irregular verbs

Base Verb	Simple Past	Past Participle
be	was, were	been
become	became	become
break	broke	broken
bring	brought	brought
build	built	built
buy	bought	bought
catch	caught	caught
choose	chose	chosen
come	came	come
cut	cut	cut
do	did	done
draw	drew	drawn
drink	drank	drunk
drive	drove	driven
eat	ate	eaten
fall	fell	fallen
feel	felt	felt
find	found	found
fit	fit	fit
fly	flew	flown
forget	forgot	forgotten
get	got	gotten
give	gave	given
go	went	gone
grow	grew	grown
hang	hung	hung
have	had	had
hear	heard	heard
hide	hid	hidden
hold	held	held
hurt	hurt	hurt
keep	kept	kept
know	knew	known
leave	left	left
lend	lent	lent
lose	lost	lost
make	made	made
meet	met	met
pay	paid	paid
put	put	put
read	read	read
ride	rode	ridden
ring	rang	rung
run	ran	run
say	said	said
see	saw	seen
sell	sold	sold
send	sent	sent
shut	shut	shut
sing	sang	sung
sit	sat	sat
sleep	slept	slept
speak	spoke	spoken
spend	spent	spent
stand	stood	stood
steal	stole	stolen
swim	swam	swum
take	took	taken
teach	taught	taught
tell	told	told
think	thought	thought
throw	threw	thrown
understand	understood	understood
wear	wore	worn
win	won	won
withdraw	withdrew	withdrawn
write	wrote	written

Credits

The authors and publishers acknowledge the following sources of copyright material and are grateful for the permissions granted. While every effort has been made, it has not always been possible to identify the sources of all the material used, or to trace all copyright holders. If any omissions are brought to our notice, we will be happy to include the appropriate acknowledgements on reprinting.

p. 2-3 (B/G): Getty Images/Lonely Planet Images; p. 3 (a): Alamy/© Imagebroker/Klaus-Werner Friedrich; p. 3 (b): Alamy/©Radius Images; p. 3 (c): Shutterstock Images/Melis; p. 3 (d): Getty Images/Chicago History Museum; p. 3 (e): Shutterstock Images/Gurgen Bakhshetsyan; p. 3 (f): Alamy/©2d Alan King; p. 3 (g): Getty Images/Retrofile/George Marks; p. 3 (h): Shutterstock Images/Ferenc Szelepcsenyi; p.3 (i): Alamy/©Bon Appetit; p. 3 (j): Shutterstock Images/Subbotina Anna; p. 3 (k): Alamy/©Greg Vaughn; p. 3 (l): Alamy/©Russell Gordon/Danita Delimont; p. 4 (BL): Corbis/Guillermo Granja; p. 4 (BR): Alamy/©Mo Fini; p. 4 (TR): Alamy/©Maria Grazia Casella; p. 5 (BR): Shutterstock Images/Blend Images; p. 6 (TL): Shutterstock Images/Jenoche/A; p. 6 (a): Shutterstock Images/James Steidl; p. 6 (b): Alamy/©Old Paper Studios; p. 6 (c): Shutterstock Images/Nataliya Hora; p. 6 (d): Shutterstock Images/Adrio Communications Ltd; p. 6 (e): Shutterstock Images/Marc Dietrich; p. 6 (f): Alamy/©Yvette Cardozo; p. 6 (g): Getty Images/De Agostini; p. 6 (h): Alamy/©Museum of London; p. 6 (i): Shutterstock Images/Balefire; p. 6 (j): Shutterstock Images/Rob Stark; p. 8 (BR): Shutterstock Images/PhotoNan; p. 8 (CL): Shutterstock Images/Doomu; p. 9 (TR): Getty Images/Adrian Weinbrecht/Digital Vision; p. 10 (B/G): Shutterstock Images/illustrart; p. 10 (TL): Getty Images/Joe Petersburger; p. 10 (TC): Getty Images/GDT; p. 10 (B): Alamy/©Chris Lewington; p. 10 (C): Alamy/©ImageDB; p. 11 (CR): Shutterstock Images/Manczurov; p. 11 (TL): Shutterstock Images/AlexMaster; p. 11 (TR): Shutterstock Images/Zybr78; p. 11 (CL): Shutterstock Images/Mike Flippo; p. 11 (CR): Shutterstock Images/WBB; p. 11 (BR): Alamy/©Urbanmyth; p. 11 (BL): Shutterstock Images/Samuel Borges Photography; p. 12-13 (B/G): Getty Images/John Eder; p. 13 (1): Getty Images/Movie Poster Image Art; p. 13 (2): Alamy/©AF Archive; p. 13 (3): ©DISNEY CHANNEL/THE KOBAL COLLECTION; p. 13 (4): REX/Courtesy Everett Collection; p. 13 (5): REX/Col Pics/Everett; p. 13 (6): Alamy/©Moviestore Collection; p. 13 (7): ©20TH CENTURY FOX/PARAMOUNT/THE KOBAL COLLECTION; p. 13 (8): REX/Courtesy Everett Collection p. 13 (9): Alamy/©AF Archive; p. 14 (T): Shutterstock Images/Bertrand Benoit; p. 14 (B/G): Shutterstock Images/Krivosheev Vitaly; p. 14 (CL): Alamy/©AF Archive; p. 14 (C): THE KOBAL COLLECTION/LUCASFILM/20TH CENTURY FOX; p. 14 (CR): Alamy/©Moviestore Collection Ltd; p. 15 (CR): Getty Images/Adrian Weinbrecht; p. 16 (TL): Shutterstock Images/Szocs Jozsef; p. 16 (1): Getty Images/Jasin Boland/NBC/NBCU Photo Bank; p. 16 (2): Alamy/©Jochen Tack; p. 16 (3): Getty Images/Steve Mort/AFP; p. 16 (4): Alamy/©AF Archive; p. 16 (5): Getty Images/Sonja Flemming/CBS; p. 16 (6): Getty Images/Alexander Tamargo; p. 16 (7): Alamy/©Pictoria Press Ltd; p. 16 (8): Alamy/©Zuma Press; p. 16 (9): Getty Images/Steve Granitz/WireImage; p. 17 (CR): Shutterstock Images/Vovan; p. 18 (TL): Shutterstock Images/Mayakova; p. 18 (BL): Alamy/©Newscast; p. 19 (B/G): Shutterstock Images/Made-in-China; p. 19 (TL): Summit Entertainment/The Kobal Collection; p. 20 (TR): Alamy/©Archives Du 7e Art/Ashutosh Gowariker Productions 12; p. 20 (CR): REX/Everett Collection; p. 20 (BR): ©DHARMA PRODUCTIONS//THE KOBAL COLLECTION; p. 20 (B/G): Shutterstock Images/Loke Yek Mang; p. 20 (TL): Shutterstock Images/Majcot; p. 21 (BR): Shutterstock Images/Kurhan; p. 22-23 (B/G): Getty Images/John Giustina; p. 23 (1): Getty Images/JupiterImages; p. 23 (2): Alamy/©Patti McConville; p. 23 (3): Alamy/©David R.Frazier; p. 23 (4): Alamy/©Alex Segre; p. 23 (5): Alamy/©Patti McConville; p. 23 (6): Alamy/©Lain Masterton; p. 23 (7): Alamy/©P.D.Amedzro; p. 23 (8): Alamy/©Jader Alto; p. 23 (9): Alamy/©Thomas Cockrem; p. 23 (10): Alamy/©Kim Kaminski; p. 23 (11): Shutterstock Images/Racorn; p. 24 (T): Alamy/©Robert Harding Picture Library Ltd; p. 24 (a): Alamy/©Caro; p. 24 (b): Alamy/©D. Hurst; p. 24 (c): Getty Images/Richard I'Anson/Lonely Planet Images; p. 24 (d): Alamy/©Laborant; p. 25 (BR): Corbis/2/Jack Hollingsworth/Ocean; p. 26 (TL): Corbis/Image Source; p. 27 (B): Shutterstock Images/Mark Poprocki; p. 28 (TL): Shutterstock Images/Dmitry Kalinovsky; p. 28 (BL): Shutterstock Images/Elnur; p. 29 (TR): Shutterstock Images/Sashkin; p. 29 (TL): Shutterstock Images/John Kasawa; p. 30 (T): Alamy/©ZUMA Press, Inc; p. 30 (C): Shutterstock Images/Dragi52; p. 30 (TR): Shutterstock Images/Joost Van Uffelen; p. 30 (B/G): Shutterstock Images/Angela Waye; p. 31 (1): Shutterstock Images/Diplomedia; p. 31 (2): Shutterstock Images/Lendy16; p. 31 (3): Alamy/©D. Hurst; p. 31 (4): Shutterstock Images/Studio Smart; p. 31 (5): Shutterstock Images/MTrebbin; p. 31 (6): Shutterstock Images/Julian Rovagnati; p. 32 (C): Corbis/Blue Images; p. 32-33 (B/G): Shutterstock Images/Neirfy; p. 33 (1): Thinkstock/mark wragg/iStock; p. 33 (2): Shutterstock Images/Brocreative; p. 33 (3): Shutterstock Images/Monika Wisniewska; p. 33 (4): Shutterstock Images/yamix; p. 33 (5): Getty Images/Maria Pereira Photograpy/Flickr; p. 33 (6): Corbis/Beau Lark; p. 33 (7): Alamy/©Shotshop GmbH; p. 33 (8): Shutterstock Images/Dmitry Yashkin; p. 33 (9): Alamy/©IE235/Image Source Plus; p. 33 (10): Shutterstock Images/mezzotint; p. 34 (TL): Getty Images/Stephen Dunn; p. 34 (TC): Getty Images/Matthew Lloyd/Bloomberg; p. 34 (TR): REX/Theo Kingma; p. 35 (TR): Alamy/©Photos 12; p. 36 (T): Shutterstock Images/Nils Petersen; p. 36 (a): Alamy/©Jack Hollingsworth/Blend Images; p. 36 (b): Shutterstock Images/Oliveromg; p. 36 (c): Alamy/©KidStock/Blend Images; p. 36 (d): Alamy/©Leah Warkentin/Design Pics Inc; p. 36 (e): Alamy/©Ron Dahlquist/Pacific Stock; p. 36 (f): Shutterstock Images/Piotr Marcinski; p. 36 (g): Alamy/©Kalle Singer/Beyond Fotomedia GmbH; p. 36 (h): Shutterstock Images/Aleksandr Markin; p. 36 (i): Alamy/©Arco Images/De Meester; p. 37 (TR): Shutterstock Images/Shvak; p. 37 (TCR): Shutterstock Images/Rarach; p. 37 (BCR): Getty Images/Image Source; p. 37 (BR): Shutterstock Images/Murengstockphoto; p. 38 (BL): Alamy/©David Grossman; p. 38 (TL): Alamy/©Rosanne Tackaberry; p. 39 (B/G): Getty Images/Jerritt Clark/Stringer; p. 39 (TL): Alamy/©Zuma Press Inc; p. 40 (TL): Getty Images/Pascal Le Segretain; p. 40 (B): Shutterstock Images/Kjersti Joergensen; p. 40 (C): Getty Images/Cameron Spencer; p. 41 (1): Shutterstock Images/Wavebreakmedia; p. 41 (2): Alamy/©PCN Photography; p. 41 (3): Shutterstock Images/Darren Baker; p. 41 (4): Alamy/©[apply pictures]; p. 42-43 (B/G): Getty Images/Marko Stavric Photography; p. 46 (T): Shutterstock Images/Mindscape Studio; p. 46 (1): Alamy/©Agencja Free; p. 46 (2): Alamy/©Blickwinkel; p. 46 (3): Shutterstock Images/Khwi; p. 46 (4): Getty images/Danita Delimont; p. 46 (5): Shutterstock Images/Catalin Petolea; p. 46 (6): Shutterstock Images/Jarry; p. 46 (7): Alamy/©Phovoir; p. 46 (8): Shutterstock Images/Golden Pixels LLC; p. 46 (9): Shutterstock Images/Gow27; p. 47 (T): Corbis/Erik Isakson/Blend Images; p. 48 (BL): Alamy/©MasPix; p. 48 (CL): Alamy/©Blickwinkel; p. 50 (TR): REX/Courtesy Everett Collection; p. 50 (CR): Getty Images/Jeff Neumann/CBS; p. 50 (B/G): Shutterstock Images/Richard Peterson; p. 54-55 (B/G): Corbis/Anna Stowe/LOOP IMAGES; p. 52-52 (B/G): Corbis/Elli Thor Magnusson; p. 56 (TL): Shutterstock Images/guentermanaus; p. 56 (CL): Alamy/©Hemis; p. 56 (TR): Shutterstock Images/Marina Jay; p. 56 (B/G): Shutterstock Images/KayaMe; p. 57 (CL): Alamy/©blickwinkel; p. 58 (TL): Getty Images/Chip Simons; p. 58 (1): Shutterstock Images/Big Pants Production; p. 58 (2): Alamy/©Incamerastock; p. 58 (3): Corbis/Ken Kaminesky/Take 2 Productions; p. 58 (4): Shutterstock Images/Shell114; p. 58 (5): Shutterstock Images/Kamil Macniak; p. 58 (6): Shutterstock Images/Ramona Heim; p. 58 (7): Shutterstock Images/Maxim Ibragimov; p. 58 (8): Shutterstock Images/Sergemi; p. 58 (9): Shutterstock Images/HomeArt; p. 58 (10): Getty Images/J.R.Ball; p. 58 (11):Shutterstock Images/Andrey Armyagov; p. 58 (12): Shutterstock Images/Africa Studio; p. 59 (CR): Shutterstock Images/Jaroslav74; p. 60 (TL): Shutterstock Images/Africa Studio; p. 60 (BL): Shutterstock Images/Gemenacom; p. 61 (TR): Shutterstock Images/Romakoma; p. 62 (T): Shutterstock Images/FCG; p. 62 (TL): Alamy/©Radius Images; p. 62 (CL): Shutterstock Images/EggHeadPhoto; p. 62 (CR): Thinkstock/Stockbyte; p. 62 (BL): Alamy/©Randy Duchaine; p. 62 (B): Shutterstock Images/View Apart; p. 64-65 (B/G): Shutterstock Images/Diversepixel; p. 65 (1): Shutterstock Images/Archiwiz; p. 65 (2): Shutterstock Images/Maksym Dykha; p. 65 (3): Shutterstock Images/AG-PHOTO; p. 65 (4): Shutterstock Images/Alexey Boldin; p. 65 (5): Alamy/©keith morris; p. 65 (6): Shutterstock Images/GeorgeMPhotography; p. 65 (7): Shutterstock Images/Joris van den Heuvel; p. 65 (8): Shutterstock Images/Bloom Design; p. 65 (9): Shutterstock Images/Goldyg; p. 66 (CR): Getty Images/SSPL; p. 66 (T): Shutterstock Images/Sergey Nivens; p. 66 (BR): Shutterstock Images/Joris van den Heuvel; p. 68 (TL): Shutterstock Images/CandyBox Images; p. 68 (a): Shutterstock Images/Showcake; p. 68 (b): Shutterstock Images/Modella; p. 68 (c): Alamy/©Pumkinpie; p. 68 (d): Shutterstock Images/Rob Marmion; p. 68 (e): Alamy/©Mark Sykes; p. 68 (f): Shutterstock Images/Valeri Potapova; p. 68 (g): Alamy/©Maxim Images; p. 69 (CR): Alamy/©Ralph Talmont/Aurora Photos; p. 70 (B): Alamy/©Peter Alvey People; p. 70 (CL): Shutterstock Images/Siberia - Video and Photo; p. 71 (TR): Shutterstock Images/Olga Popova; p. 72 (TL): Shutterstock Images/James Steidl; p. 72 (BR): Alamy/©Ian Dagnall Computing; p. 72 (TR): Shutterstock Images/Fad82; p. 72 (BL): Shutterstock Images/Kitch Bain; p. 72 (B/G): Shutterstock Images/Concept Photo; p. 73 (1): Shutterstock Images/Luis Carlos Torres; p. 73 (2): Shutterstock Images/Maksym Dykha; p. 73 (3): Shutterstock Images/BigKnell; p. 73 (4): Shutterstock Images/Volodymyr Krasyuk; p. 74-75 (B/G): Corbis/Werner Dieterich/Westend61; p. 75 (a): Shutterstock Images/Monkey Business Images; p. 75 (b): Alamy/©Driver's License; p. 75 (c): Alamy/©Cultura Creative; p. 75 (d): Shutterstock Images/Nikola Solev; p. 75 (e): Shutterstock Images/razihusin; p. 75 (f): Shutterstock Images/Joe Gough; p. 75 (g): Shutterstock Images/Karen Grigoryan; p. 75 (h): Alamy/©Ben Molyneux People; p. 75 (i): Corbis/Mark Edward Atkinson/Tracey Lee/Blend Images; p. 75 (j): Shutterstock Images/Monkey Business Images; p. 76 (TL): REX/Bruce Adams;p. 76 (TC): Alamy/©Bill Bachman; p. 77 (BL): Shutterstock Images/MTrebbin; p. 77 (TL): Shutterstock Images/GeniusKp; p. 77 (TR): Shutterstock Images/Arman Zhenikeyev; p. 77 (BR): Shutterstock Images/Irin-k; p. 78 (T): Alamy/©VStock; p. 78 (1): Shutterstock Images/Carsten Reisinger; p. 78 (2): Shutterstock Images/Rob Hyrons; p. 78 (3): Shutterstock Images/Molodec; p. 78 (4): Shutterstock Images/jocic; p. 78 (5): Shutterstock Images/Worker; p. 78 (6): Shutterstock Images/R. Gino Santa Maria; p. 78 (7): Shutterstock Images/Nikkytok; p. 78 (8): Shutterstock Images/Donatas1205; p. 79 (BR): Getty images/Muammer Mujdat Uzel; p. 80 (TL): Shutterstock Images/Bloomua; p. 80 (BL): Alamy/©Denise Hager Catchlight Visual Services; p. 81 (TR): Getty Images/Juanmonino; p. 82 (BL): Alamy/©Steve Skjold; p. 82 (CL): Alamy/©Alaska Stock; p. 82 (B/G): Shutterstock Images/Galyna Andrushko; p. 82 (TL): Alamy/©Gail Mooney-Kelly; p. 82 (T): Shutterstock Images/Galyna Andrushko; p. 83 (1): Shutterstock Images/Roman Samokhin; p. 83 (2): Shutterstock Images/Hal_P; p. 83 (3): Shutterstock Images/EZeePics Studio; p. 83 (4): Alamy/©Mike Kemp; p. 84-85 (B/G): Corbis/Corey Rich/Aurora Open; p .85 (1): Getty Images/Tammy Bryngelson; p. 85 (2): Alamy/©Rob Stark; p. 85 (3): Shutterstock Images/Apples Eyes Studio; p. 85 (4): Alamy/©Nik Taylor; p. 85 (5): Shutterstock Images/Robert Crum; p. 85 (6): Alamy/©Imagebroker; p. 85 (7): Getty Images/Jason Weddington; p. 85 (8): Corbis/Burger/phanie/Phanie Sarl; p. 85 (9): Shutterstock Images/Piotr Marcinski; p. 85 (10): Shutterstock Images/Mahathir Mohd Yasin; p. 86 (CR): Alamy/©Trekandshoot; p. 86 (TR): Shutterstock Images/Dan Thornberg; p. 86 (TL): Shutterstock Images/Ilya Andriyanov; p. 86 (CL): Shutterstock Images/Filatov Alexey; p. 86 (T): Shutterstock Images/Endeavor; p. 87 (CR): Getty Images/Ebby May; p. 88 (T): Shutterstock Images/Varuna; p. 88 (BL): Alamy/©Image Source Plus; p. 88 (BC): Alamy/©Enigma; p. 89 (BR): REX/Andrew Price; p. 90 (TL): Shutterstock Images/Wonderisland; p. 90 (BL): Shutterstock Images/HomeArt; p. 91 (TR): Shutterstock Images/Stefan Pircher; p. 92 (TL): Shutterstock Images/Dr.Morley Read; p. 92 (TC): Shutterstock Images/Kletr; p. 92 (BR): Shutterstock Images/Decha Thapanya; p. 92 (T): Shutterstock Images/Foxy; p. 92 (B/G): Shutterstock Images/Brodtcast; p. 92 (BL): Alamy/©Robert M. Vera; p. 92 (TR): Getty Images/Murray Cooper/Minden Pictures; p. 93 (1,2,3,4): Shutterstock Images/Goa Novi; p. 93 (5,6,7): Shutterstock Images/Flashon Studio; p. 93 (8,9): Shutterstock Images/Iko; p. 94-95 (B/G): Corbis/Tim Pannell; p. 95 (1): Shutterstock Images/Claudia Paulussen; p. 95 (2): Shutterstock Images/Golden Pixels LLC; p. 95 (3): Getty Images/Jupiter Images; p. 95 (4): Shutterstock Images/Christine Langer-Pueschel; p. 95 (5): Shutterstock Images/BlueSkyImage; p. 95 (6): Alamy/©Radius Images; p. 95 (7): Alamy/©Frederic Cirou/PhotoAlto sas; p. 95 (8): Getty Images/Rob Lewine; p. 96 (TL): Alamy/©Zuma Press Inc; p. 96 (TC): Getty Images/Fuse; p. 96 (TR): Alamy/©Gregory James; p. 97 (CL): Alamy/©South West Images Scotland; p. 98 (TL): Getty Images/Mbbirdy; p. 98 (1): Shutterstock Images/PathDoc; p. 98 (2): Shutterstock Images/Guillermo Del Olmo; p. 98 (3): Shutterstock Images/Patrick Foto; p. 98 (4): Shutterstock Images/PathDoc; p. 98 (5): Shutterstock Images/Arvydas Kniuksta; p. 98 (6): Shutterstock Images/Sabphoto; p. 98 (7): Shutterstock Images/Sashahaltam; p. 98 (8): Shutterstock Images/Tracy Whiteside; p. 98 (9): Shutterstock Images/Elena Elisseeva; p. 98 (10): Shutterstock Images/Jeka; p. 100 (TL): Getty Images/Nancy R.Cohen; p. 100 (BL): Getty Images/SW Productions/Photodisc; p. 101 (TR): Alamy/©View Pictures Ltd; p. 102 (B): Shutterstock Images/Roman Sigaev; p. 102 (TR): Shutterstock Images/Focuslight; p. 103 (1): Shutterstock Images/Denise Kappa; p. 103 (2): Shutterstock Images/Studio Vin; p. 103 (3): Alamy/©Niehoff/Imagebroker; p. 103 (4): Shutterstock Images/Taelove7; p. 103 (5): Shutterstock Images/ Artiis; p. 103 (6): Shutterstock Images/Aerogondo2; p. 104-105 (B/G): Shutterstock Images/Alexander Vershinin; p. 116 (T): Getty Images/Javier Pierini; p. 117 (T): Shutterstock Images/Jktu_21; Back cover: Shutterstock Images/Vibrant Image Studio.

Front cover photography by Alamy/©Marc Hill.

The publishers are grateful to the following illustrators:

David Belmonte p. 44; Nigel Dobbyn p. 43, 49, 102; Q2A Media Services, Inc. p. 7, 55, 63, 118;
Jose Rubio p. 26, 119; Sean Tiffany p. 7.

All video stills by kind permission of:

Discovery Communications, LLC 2015: p. 2 (1, 3), 5, 10, 12 (1, 3, 4), 15, 20, 21, 22 (1, 3), 25, 30, 32 (1, 3, 4), 35, 40, 41, 42 (1, 3, 4), 45, 50, 51, 54 (1, 3), 57, 62, 64 (1, 3, 4), 67, 72, 73, 74 (1, 3), 77, 82, 84 (1, 3), 87, 92, 94 (1, 3, 4), 97, 102, 103, 116, 117, 118, 119, 120; Cambridge University Press: p. 2 (2), 8, 12 (2), 18, 22 (2), 28, 32 (2), 38, 42 (2), 48, 54 (2), 60, 64 (2), 70, 72 (2), 80, 84 (2), 90, 94 (2), 100.

Credits

The authors and publishers acknowledge the following sources of copyright material and are grateful for the permissions granted. While every effort has been made, it has not always been possible to identify the sources of all the material used, or to trace all copyright holders. If any omissions are brought to our notice, we will be happy to include the appropriate acknowledgements on reprinting.

p.3 (TL): Shutterstock Images/Sergiyn; p.5 (TR): Alamy/©The Photolibrary Wales/Steve Benbow; p. 10 (1): Getty Images/Steve Granitz/WireImage; p. 10 (2): Getty Images/Sonja Flemming/CBS; p. 10 (3): Alamy/©ZUMA Press; p. 10 (4): Getty Images/Steve MORT/AFP; p. 10 (5): Getty Images/Jasin Boland/NBC/NBCU Photo Bank; p. 10 (6): Getty Images/Alexander Tamargo; p. 10 (7): Alamy/©Jochen Tack; p. 10 (8): Alamy/©Pictorial Press Ltd; p. 10 (9): Alamy/©AF archive; p. 11 (TL): Alamy/©Blend Images/Jeff Greenough; p. 14 (CL): Shutterstock Images/FXQuadro; p. 18 (CL): Alamy/©Daniel Dempster Photography; p. 27 (TL): Alamy/©Everett Collection Inc; p. 33 (TR): Alamy/©Megapress; p. 37 (CR): Alamy/©Andreas Von Einsiedel; p. 39 (TL): Shutterstock Images/Julian Rovagnati; p. 47 (TL): Shutterstock Images/Ermolaev Alexander; p. 50 (1): Alamy/©MBI; p. 50 (2): Getty Images/Jupiterimages; p. 50 (3): Shutterstock Images/Michaeljung; p. 50 (4): Shutterstock Images/Pierdelune; p. 50 (5): Getty Images/MachineHeadz; p. 50 (6): Shutterstock Images/Denis Kukareko; p. 50 (7): Alamy/©Jim West; p. 50 (8): Shutterstock Images/oliveromg; p. 50 (9): Alamy/©age fotostock Spain, S.L.; p. 50 (10): Shutterstock Images/Sofia Andreevna; p. 51 (BL): Alamy/©Andres Rodriguez; p.53 (BL): Shutterstock Images/Mariyana M; p.53 (BC): Alamy/©Oote Boe 3; p. 56 (1): Shutterstock Images/Africa Studio; p. 56 (2): Shutterstock Images/Roadk; p. 56 (3): Shutterstock Images/Photosync; p. 56 (4): Shutterstock Images/Veronchick84; p. 56 (5): Shutterstock Images/Stephen Mcsweeny; p. 56 (6): Shutterstock Images/Africa Studio; p. 56 (7): Shutterstock Images/R.Legosyn; p. 56 (8): Shutterstock Images/Kellie L.Folkerts; p. 56 (9): Shutterstock Images/Liu Anlin; p. 56 (10): Shutterstock Images/MichaelJay Berlin; p. 56 (11): Getty Images/Wavebreak Media; p. 59 (CL): Shutterstock Images/PhotoSky; p. 63 (TR): Alamy/©Purcell Team; p. 64 (BL): Getty Images/Tim Hall; Back cover: Shutterstock Images/Vibrant Image Studio.

Front cover photograph by Alamy/©Marc Hill.

The publishers are grateful to the following illustrators:

Janet Allinger p. 6, 32, 54; Galia Bernstein p. 19, 25, 26, 31, 40, 41, 45, 55, 66 (TR), 67, 70; Anni Betts p. 2, 21, 28, 30, 60, 61, 68; Alberto de Hoyos p. 22 (1-5, 7, 9, 10), 58 (1-10); Nigel Dobbyn p. 4, 8, 48, 52 (TR), 62; Mark Duffin p. 44 (1-3, 5-7); Simon Ecob p. 9, 14, 15, 17, 24, 35; Q2A Media Services, Inc. p. 7, 19, 25, 26, 31, 40, 41, 44 (4), 45, 46, 52 (TL), 55, 65, 66, 67, 70; Jose Rubio p. 12, 13, 20, 22 (6, CR), 34, 42, 43, 58 (C); David Shephard p. 36; Norbert Sipos p. 38, 49.

All video stills by kind permission of Discovery Communications, LLC 2015.

Notes

Notes

Notes